ROUTLEDGE LIBRARY EDITIONS:
EXCHANGE RATE ECONOMICS

Volume 7

EXPECTATIONS AND THE FOREIGN EXCHANGE MARKET

EXPECTATIONS AND THE FOREIGN EXCHANGE MARKET

CRAIG S. HAKKIO

Routledge
Taylor & Francis Group

LONDON AND NEW YORK

First published in 1984 by Garland Publishing, Inc.

This edition first published in 2017
by Routledge
2 Park Square, Milton Park, Abingdon, Oxon OX14 4RN

and by Routledge
711 Third Avenue, New York, NY 10017

Routledge is an imprint of the Taylor & Francis Group, an informa business

British Library Cataloguing in Publication Data
A catalogue record for this book is available from the British Library

ISBN: 978-0-415-79325-4 (Set)
ISBN: 978-1-315-21117-6 (Set) (ebk)
ISBN: 978-1-138-63322-3 (Volume 7) (hbk)
ISBN: 978-1-315-20778-0 (Volume 7) (ebk)

Publisher's Note
The publisher has gone to great lengths to ensure the quality of this reprint but
points out that some imperfections in the original copies may be apparent.

Disclaimer
The publisher has made every effort to trace copyright holders and would welcome
correspondence from those they have been unable to trace.

Expectations and the Foreign Exchange Market

Craig S. Hakkio

Garland Publishing, Inc.
New York & London, 1984

Library of Congress Cataloging in Publication Data

Hakkio, Craig S. (Craig Stephan), 1952–
    Expectations and the foreign exchange market.

    (Outstanding dissertations in economics)
    Originally presented as the author's thesis (Ph.D.)—
University of Chicago, 1979.
    Bibliography: p.
    1. Forward exchange—Mathematical models.   I. Title.
II. Series.
HG3853.H34   1984   332.4'566   80-8627
ISBN 0-8240-4184-4

All volumes in this series are printed on acid-free,
250-year-life paper.

Printed in the United States of America

THE UNIVERSITY OF CHICAGO

EXPECTATIONS AND THE FOREIGN EXCHANGE MARKET

A DISSERTATION SUBMITTED TO

THE FACULTY OF THE DIVISION OF THE SOCIAL SCIENCES

IN CANDIDACY FOR THE DEGREE OF

DOCTOR OF PHILOSOPHY

DEPARTMENT OF ECONOMICS

BY

CRAIG S. HAKKIO

CHICAGO, ILLINOIS

DECEMBER 1979

TABLE OF CONTENTS

ACKNOWLEDGMENTS

I would like to thank the members of my dissertation committee, Professors Robert E. Lucas, Jr., Michael Mussa and Gary R. Skoog, for their help in writing this dissertation. In particular, I would like to thank my chairman, Professor Jacob A. Frenkel, for his constant help and encouragement. I would also like to thank my father, John A. Hakkio, my sister, Joan H. Kerr, and the rest of my family for their continued support. Finally, I would like to thank Alyce G. Monroe for her excellent job of typing this dissertation.

LIST OF TABLES

CHAPTER I

INTRODUCTION

1.1 Introduction

The apparently erratic behavior of exchange rates over the last six
years led many international macroeconomists to re-examine the theories of
exchange rate determination. This recent research led to theories that focus
on asset markets and the role played by expectations about the future values
of exogenous variables. A major conclusion of this theory is that exchange
rates are expected to fluctuate in response to new information reaching the
foreign exchange market. Two of the main questions which have been the subject of recent research are: (i) what should be the extent of exchange rate
fluctuations, and (ii) have exchange rates fluctuated too much? In analyzing
these questions, the assumption that expectations represent optimal forecasts and that, broadly speaking, foreign exchange markets behave like other
asset markets provides a convenient norm: if exchange rate forecast errors
(correctly defined to allow for the known structure of the economy, for
example by allowing for a constant risk premium) cannot be explained by information readily available to the market, then the foreign exchange market is
said to be efficient. With this norm, the "erratic" behavior of exchange
rates is a reflection of the situation in which new information coming to the
market is quickly incorporated into exchange rates.

This dissertation examines two important dimensions of efficiency
in the foreign exchange market using new econometric techniques.   The

1

first dimension of efficiency that is examined is the relation between spot and forward exchange rates. In particular, does the forward rate summarize all relevant and available information concerning the future values of the spot rate? The second dimension of efficiency that is examined is the term structure of the forward premium. We observe that forward contracts of many maturities are simultaneously traded in the foreign exchange market. Do the various maturities move in a manner consistent with economic theory? The particular aspect of the theory of the term structure on which we.will focus is whether the six month forward premium can be written as a geometric average of expected one month forward premiums. Both dimensions of efficiency require a joint test of market efficiency and the equilibrium model being used. A rejection of any such test may, therefore, represent a rejection of market efficiency, or a rejection of the particular model being used, or both.

Chapter II of this dissertation provides an extensive examination of the hypothesis that the forward rate provides an "optimal" forecast of the future spot rate. This hypothesis is analyzed using two distinct, but related, approaches. The first, and more traditional, approach is based on a regression of spot rates on lagged forward rates. One of the novel features in this analysis is the use of weekly data with a one month forward rate. In using weekly data and a one month forward exchange rate, one must realize that the forecasting horizon (one month) exceeds the sampling interval (one week). Under these conditions, ordinary least squares regression analysis of market efficiency is incorrect. The difficulty arises due to the combination of the error term having a (known) time series representation and the forward rate being a lagged endogenous variable. This study analyzes the implications of this difficulty for the traditional

regression analysis of market efficiency. Econometric methods are used
which allow for consistent (though not fully efficient) estimation of the
parameters and their standard errors.

Chapter II also presents a novel approach to testing this first
dimension of exchange market efficiency. This new approach is based on an
explicit time series analysis of the spot and forward rates. It allows
for a more (econometrically) efficient procedure that uses the structure
of the serial correlation of the errors in estimating the parameters. A
general (bivariate) time series process for the spot and forward exchange
rate is employed in which these rates are simultaneously determined. This
procedure allows us to extract an optimal forecast of the future spot rate.
The hypothesis of efficiency is now viewed as a set of cross-equation restrictions imposed on the parameters of the time series model. Chapter II
will derive these restrictions, propose a maximum likelihood method of estimating the constrained and unconstrained likelihood function, estimate the
model and then test the validity of the restrictions with a likelihood
ratio statistic.

We shall find that the standard regression methods yield results
that are marginally favorable to the hypothesis of efficiency. In particular, it will be shown that, for the period April 1973 to May 1977, the
forward rate is an unbiased forecast of the future spot rate for Canada,
Switzerland and the United Kingdom; the forward rate is a biased forecast
of the future spot rate for the Netherlands and Germany. In addition, for
the Netherlands, Germany and Switzerland the forward rate appears to summarize all available information about the future value of the spot rate,
while for Canada and the U.K. there appears to be relevant information in
the residuals that is not captured by the forward rate. The time series

4

approach indicates rejection of efficiency for all five currencies. The
cause for the rejection is difficult to ascertain. In addition, we must
recall that we are always testing a joint hypothesis.

The second dimension of efficiency that is examined arises from
the observation that forward contracts exist for various maturities. When
various maturities for a given currency exist, we expect there to be a time
series relationship between these various forward rates. In Chapter III an
equilibrium model describing the term structure of the forward premium will
be developed. This theory will combine the pure expectations theory of the
term structure of (domestic and foreign) interest rates with the hypothesis
of interest rate parity which states that interest rate differentials reflect
expected exchange rate depreciation. The theory is developed such that the
model and its implications can be empirically tested The empirical specification is based on a time series analysis of the one and six month forward
premiums. A general bivariate time series representation is postulated for
the one and six month forward premiums. The theory of the term structure
of the forward premium will impose testable cross equation restrictions on
the parameters of the model. Two distinct statistical tests are used to
test the validity of the restrictions. Although the tests are asymptotically
equivalent, we can not compare them in finite samples. One test requires
simply the unconstrained estimates while the other test also requires the
constrained estimates.

Chapter III examines the German and Canadian term structure of the
forward premium for the period April 1973 to December 1976. For Germany,
the data are consistent with the model proposed, while for Canada the data
are inconsistent with the model. From an econometric point of view, the
interesting result is that both tests yield identical conclusions.

As indicated earlier, the standard ordinary least squares procedures, with weekly data and a one month forward rate, yield consistent,
though not fully efficient, parameter estimates and incorrect standard
errors. It is possible to modify these procedures to obtain consistent
estimates of the standard errors. To obtain efficient estimates we develop a new time series procedure. Chapters II and III discuss and apply
this new procedure to the study of efficiency in the foreign exchange
market. The unifying theme underlying the two hypotheses to be tested is
that certain variables can be used to forecast future values of other
variables: the forward rate is used to forecast the future spot rate and
the forward premium is used to forecast the expected rate of depreciation.
Let x_1 and x_2 represent the two variables of interest (spot and forward
rate, one and six month forward premiums). We assume that $\{x_{1,t}, x_{2,t}\}$ is
generated by a bivariate vector autoregression. That is, we regress both
$x_{1,t}$ and $x_{2,t}$ on lagged values of themselves. Next, economic theory relates
current values of, say, $x_{1,t}$, with future values of $x_{2,t}$. The hypothesis
of rational expectations implies that economic agents in forecasting future
values of x_2 will use the structure of the model (the parameters of the bivariate autoregression, in this case) and the relevant economic theory. In
the multi-period forecasts considered here, agents will use the "chain rule
of forecasting," which provides a convenient method for calculating expectations of $x_{2,t}$ arbitrarily far into the future from knowledge of the one-
step ahead forecasts. Not only is this method convenient, but it also em-
ploys fully all information available to the agents. For the data to be
consistent with the model, the parameters of the autoregression must be
restricted. The form of the restrictions can be developed and tested using
maximum likelihood methods.

There has been much written on the subject of foreign exchange market efficiency using the standard regression methods. Section 1.2 will briefly summarize this literature. Finally, Section 1.3 will discuss the currencies to be used and present a summary of the economic conditions in the various countries during the period in question.

1.2 Review of the Literature

Since a number of excellent surveys of the literature on exchange rate behavior already exist (Levich 1978, 1979 and Kohlhagen), I will focus on the more recent work concerning market efficiency and the term structure of the forward premium.

To determine if exchange rate movements are excessive, one needs to define a norm. In an efficient market, prices are said to "fully reflect" all available information (Fama 1969). In the foreign exchange market, there are two (domestic) prices of foreign exchange that are of interest: (1) the spot exchange rate (S_t), the price today for delivery today, and (2) the forward exchange rate (F_t^τ), the price today for delivery τ periods in the future. Both S_t and F_t^τ reflect the price of foreign exchange today, but for delivery at different points in time. If prices do reflect all information, then one would expect F_t^τ to summarize all information concerning the price of foreign exchange at time $t+\tau$, $S_{t+\tau}$, that is available today. The expected value of $S_{t+\tau}$, given information up to time t, should be a function of F_t^τ. In a world of uncertainty about nominal and real variables, and risk neutral agents, one would expect that $E(S_{t+\tau} : I_t) = F_t^\tau$, where $E(x_s : I_t)$ indicates the expectation of x for time s, conditional on information up to (and including) time t. However, if agents are risk averse, one would not expect the forward rate to be an unbiased predictor of the future (random) spot rate (see, for example, Stockman 1978, Roll-Solnick 1977, and Kouri 1976). In such a case, a risk premium will be present,[1] and the relation may be a linear function:

$$E(S_{t+\tau} : I_t) = a + bF_t^{\tau} \qquad (1.1)$$

In equation (1.1), the risk premium can take two forms: either the intercept can differ from zero ($a \neq 0$), or the slope coefficient can differ from unity ($b \neq 1$). The case of $a \neq 0$ is the usual notion of a constant risk premium (see Stockman 1978 for an example of constraining $b = 1$ and allowing a to be free). If the risk premium results in $a \neq 0$ and $b \neq 1$, then we can rewrite (1.1) as:

$$E(S_{t+\tau} : I_t) - F_t^{\tau} = a + (b-1)F_t^{\tau} \qquad (1.2)$$

The left hand side of (1.2) being negative (so that $E(S_{t+\tau} : I_t) < F_t$) corresponds to the situation of dollars being riskier than foreign currency. That is, the buyer of forward foreign currency is willing to purchase forward foreign currency at a higher price than the spot price expected to prevail in the future. The right hand side of (1.2) gives an expression

---

[1]The concept of a premium in the foreign exchange market is very delicate. We know that, in general, when agents are risk averse a risk premium, reflecting the concavity of the utility function, will arise. This is to be distinguished from Jensen's inequality which is solely a property of probability distribution functions (see Stockman 1978 for such an analysis and decomposition). However, when both sides of the market are risk averse, we cannot a priori sign the risk premium. Fama and Farber (1978) consider a world with money, nominal bonds and uncertainty about future price levels and hence different purchasing power risks of the monies. In such a world, internationally traded nominal bonds means that "the purchasing power of a country's money supply is [not] borne entirely by its residents" (Fama and Farber 1978, p. 15). When strict purchasing power parity also holds, there is no independent exchange rate risk. This does not mean that forward rates will not "still contain premiums or discounts vis-a-vis predictions of futue spot exchange rates" (Fama and Farber 1978, p. 18). The premium will reflect different purchasing power risks of the monies of the two countries.

for the amount of the premium (or discount); it is seen to be expressed
as the sum of a constant (a) and a fraction of F_t^τ $\left((b-a)F_t^\tau\right)$.

Expressing a risk premium as $a + (b-1)F_t^\tau$ does not initially appear
satisfactory. This would seem to imply that countries with a higher level
of the forward exchange rate would have a larger risk premium. This would
clearly be unsatisfactory. A more satisfactory interpretation is to think
of a and b as being specific to a country. Then, $a + (b-1)F_t^\tau$ representing
the risk premium means that for a given level of the exchange rate, the higher
the value of F_t^τ the larger the risk premium. Interpreted this way, we have
that for a given value of S_t, a larger value of F_t^τ represents a larger
forward premium, which is then positively related to the magnitude of the
risk premium.

In the past, most researchers used monthly data, preferring to
ignore the complications arising from the use of weekly data. Recently,
researchers have begun to use weekly data (Stockman 1978, Obstfeld 1978,
Garber 1978, and Hansen and Hodrick 1979). Both Stockman and Hansen and
Hodrick focus on the forecast errors, $\ln S_t - \ln F_{t-k}$ (k = 4 for Stockman
and k = 13 for Hansen and Hodrick). Stockman provides efficient estimates
of both the constant term (risk premium) and the parameters of the time
series process generating the forecast error. Hansen and Hodrick test if
there exist variables available to the market that could help explain the
forecast errors. The variables they use are lagged (own) forecast errors
and forecast errors made with other currencies. They are able to test the
significance of these other variables after providing consistent estimates
of both the parameters and their associated standard errors.

Forward contracts in foreign currencies are currently being traded
with maturities of 1, 2, 3, 6, 9 and 12 month maturities. Most studies

have focused on a single maturity. Few authors have examined the entire

spectrum of maturities. Three studies have examined the term structure

of the forward premium--Porter (1971), Giddy (1977) and Brillembourg (1978).

The first two papers concentrate on the interrelationships between

the term structure of the ratio of international interest rates and exchange

rate expectations, relating the two quantities by interest rate parity.

Both papers assume a certainty equivalent framework for the term structure.

Both analyze the implications of exchange rate expectations for the term

structure of interest rates, and, the term structure of interest rates for

exchange rate expectations. Porter(1971) shows that the term structure of

international interest rate ratios can be decomposed into a geometric average

of expected exchange rate changes. Giddy (1977) generalizes this theory

by allowing liquidity premiums for the term structure of domestic interest

rates, foreign interest rates and exchange rates.

Brillembourg (1978) focuses on the forecast revision of the forward

rate: $\ln F_t^n - \ln F_{t-1}^{n+1}$. He is able to decompose this quantity into three

components: "(a) a constant term which is the difference betwen the risk

premium for one and n weeks ahead; (b) the error made in forecasting the

current spot rate and (c) an error term which need not be serially uncorre-

lated" (Brillembourg 1978, p. 12). Using this model, Brillembourg is able

to estimate a risk premium curve for Canada and the U.K. The curve has a

humped shape, starting at zero for short maturities, rising to 4.0 basis

points per week for contracts with a maturity of 30-40 weeks, and then

declining to about 2.0 bases points per week for contracts with a maturity

of 52 weeks.

Much work has been done on the term structure of interest rates.

Two that are of special interest are Modigliani-Shiller (1973) and
Sargent (1978). In the paper by Modigliani-Shiller they regress the long
rate on lagged values of the short rate. Such a model is consistent with
the theory of optimal linear least squares prediction. Sargent (1978), on
the other hand, does not limit himself to regressing the long rate on past
short rates alone, instead, he considers a bivariate autoregression of short
and long rates. The advantage of this is that this "conserves all of the
information required to compute the projection of one interest rate series
on current and past (and maybe future) values of the other series" (Sargent
1978, p. 2).

1.3 Description of the Data

Five exchange rates (with respect to the dollar) will be examined.
These currencies are (1) the Dutch guilder (the Netherlands), (2) the German
mark, (3) the Canadian dollar, (4) the Swiss franc and (5) the U.K. pound.
The period to be analyzed is April 24, 1973 to May 5, 1977. The ending date
was arbitrary, while the starting date reflected the fact that there ap-
peared to be a structural change in the international monetary system in
March 1973, when the EEC agreement to stabilize the dollar value of their
currencies within a 2.25 percent band was abandoned (see Frenkel 1978,
Frenkel-Levich 1977, and Levich 1977 for evidence on this observation).
Weekly observations were obtained (from the International Monetary Market
Yearbook) on bid spot and one month forward rates on the New York foreign
exchange market. Forward rates are (generally) observed on Tuesdays, while
spot rates are observed on Thursdays. The reason for this staggering of
observations is that one month is equal to (approximately) four weeks and
two days.

The countries chosen are all industrialized countries with well-integrated capital and foreign exchange markets. The countries are, however, diverse in terms of their economic experiences over the sample period. Table 1 presents some summary statistics. We shall be interested in the behavior of the international monetary system over time, consequently, growth rates for selected economic time series for the period as a whole and for each of the two subperiods are calculated. For the entire period, April 1973-May 1977, only the U.K. had a negative growth rate of industrial production, -0.66 percent per year. However, these results may be slightly misleading since the growth rates for the first period, April 1973-April 1975, are generally substantially different from those of the second period, May 1975-May 1977. During the early period most countries experienced a drop in industrial production while experiencing a rise in industrial production in the later period. A similar story is seen in looking at the growth rates of real GNP. The six countries show a large range in rates of monetary growth, from a low of 2.95 percent for Switzerland to a high of 12.5 percent for the Netherlands. Similarly, the rates of price inflation vary from 5.09 percent for Switzerland to 18.09 percent for the U.K. The rates of monetary growth increase in going from early to late period, while the rates of inflation decrease.

Table 2 presents various measures of exchange rate volatility for the whole period and each subperiod. In general we find that the rate of depreciation, the forward premium and forecast error are insignificantly different from zero. For example, the U.K. pound depreciated relative to the dollar by 0.807 percent per month, which translates to 9.7 percent per year, with a standard deviation of 0.289 percent per month, for the period April 1973 to May 1977. For the two subperiods, the U.K. pound depreciated

TABLE 1

GROWTH RATES OF SELECTED ECONOMIC TIME SERIES

Period	Country	Industrial Production	Real GNP	Money	Prices
April 1973– May 1977	United States	1.54	1.82	5.00	8.22
	Netherlands	2.38	--	12.58	9.07
	Germany	0.09	1.40	8.20	5.59
	Canada	1.45	3.30	7.04	9.44
	Switzerland	--	--	2.95	5.09
	United Kingdom	-0.66	0.16	12.50	18.09
April 1973– April 1975	United States	-6.16	-1.38	4.80	10.07
	Netherlands	0.49	--	6.19	10.01
	Germany	-4.45	-0.94	6.45	6.66
	Canada	-1.14	2.52	7.00	10.61
	Switzerland	--	--	0.11	8.71
	United Kingdom	-4.21	-1.28	9.48	18.50
May 1975– May 1977	United States	9.82	5.51	5.21	6.39
	Netherlands	4.30	--	19.31	8.15
	Germany	4.82	4.09	9.97	4.53
	Canada	4.09	4.18	7.07	8.28
	Switzerland	--	--	5.87	1.58
	United Kingdom	3.00	1.80	15.59	17.68

NOTES: The growth rate for industrial production, money and price were calculated as the annualized rate of change based on monthly data. The growth rate for real GNP (in 1975 currency) was calculated as the annualized rate of change based on monthly data. Price data was the CPI. All data was obtained from the IFS (International Financial Statistics).

13

TABLE 2

SIMPLE MEASURES OF EXCHANGE RATE VOLATILITY

Period	Country	Rate of Depreciation	Forward Premium	Forecast Error	$Var(\ln S_t)$
April 1973– May 1975	Netherlands	0.00184 (0.00388)	-0.00128 (0.00107)	0.00312 (0.00387)	0.00222
	Germany	0.00147 (0.00411)	0.00001 (0.00089)	0.00145 (0.00421)	0.00205
	Canada	-0.00131 (0.00160)	-0.00145 (0.00056)	0.00140 (0.00174)	0.00050
	Switzerland	0.00368 (0.00391)	0.00039 (0.00118)	0.00330 (0.00403)	0.00849
	United Kingdom	-0.00807 (0.00289)	-0.00553 (0.00094)	-0.00255 (0.00332)	0.01937
April 1973– April 1975	Netherlands	0.00473 (0.00690)	-0.00130 (0.00199)	0.00603 (0.00658)	0.00274
	Germany	0.00312 (0.00751)	-0.00049 (0.00150)	0.00361 (0.00758)	0.00268
	Canada	-0.00139 (0.00171)	0.00008 (0.00079)	-0.00147 (0.00164)	0.00021
	Switzerland	0.00724 (0.00745)	-0.00079 (0.00205)	0.00804 (0.00753)	0.00712
	United Kingdom	-0.00366 (0.00356)	-0.00507 (0.00162)	0.00140 (0.00447)	0.00092
May 1975– May 1977	Netherlands	-0.00120 (0.00427)	-0.00120 (0.00104)	-0.00000 (0.00473)	0.00135
	Germany	-0.00067 (0.00424)	0.00096 (0.00104)	-0.00163 (0.00448)	0.00132
	Canada	-0.00092 (0.00287)	-0.00306 (0.00073)	0.00214 (0.00318)	0.00064
	Switzerland	-0.00051 (0.00316)	0.00216 (0.00125)	-0.00267 (0.00342)	0.00095
	United Kingdom	-0.01163 (0.00459)	-0.00563 (0.00108)	-0.00600 (0.00524)	0.00999

NOTES: All exchange rates are measured on the first week of each month in terms of the U.S. dollar. A positive number reflects a depreciation of the U.S. dollar, on a monthly basis. The rate of depreciation is the average rate, calculated as a simple average of $\ln S_{t-4} - \ln S_t$; the forward premium is the average forward premium, calculated as a simple average of $\ln F_t - \ln S_t$. The standard deviation of the average is reported in parentheses.

at the rate of 0.366 per cent per month and 1.163 percent per month. We also notice that the standard deviation of the average forward premium is substantially less than the standard deviation for the average rate of depreciation.

Two of the exchange rate series of interest are the spot rate and one month forward rate, observed on a weekly basis. In the statistical work we shall work with the logarithms of the variables. Tables 3-5 show the autocorrelation function (up to order 24) of $\ln S_t$, $\ln F_t$ and the forecast error, $\ln S_t - \ln F_{t-4}$. The autocorrelation function $\rho(k)$ (estimated by $r(k)$) is defined as $[E(x_t-\mu)(x_{t-k}-\mu)/E(x_t-\mu)(x_t-\mu)]$. A knowledge of the autocorrelation function will provide information about the time series path for a variable and will allow for comparisons between series. The major conclusion to be drawn from the autocorrelation functions of $\ln S_t$ and $\ln F_t$ is that each series appears to be nonstationary. This is seen by noting that the autocorrelation function dies out very slowly. The autocorrelation function of the forecast error indicates that $\ln S_t - \ln F_{t-4}$ is probably a moving average process of order four. This is seen by noting that the first four autocorrelations are significantly different from zero, while the rest are (generally) insignificantly different from zero. As will be seen later, this is what the theory would predict.

TABLE 3

AUTOCORRELATIONS OF $\ln S_t$

(April 1973 – May 1977)

Country	r_1 / r_{13}	r_2 / r_{14}	r_3 / r_{15}	r_4 / r_{16}	r_5 / r_{17}	r_6 / r_{18}	r_7 / r_{19}	r_8 / r_{20}	r_9 / r_{21}	r_{10} / r_{22}	r_{11} / r_{23}	r_{12} / r_{24}	s.e.
Netherlands	0.96	0.91	0.85	0.79	0.73	0.68	0.63	0.58	0.54	0.50	0.45	0.40	0.07
	0.34	0.29	0.24	0.19	0.15	0.11	0.08	0.05	0.04	0.02	0.01	-0.01	0.24
Germany	0.95	0.89	0.83	0.75	0.69	0.63	0.57	0.51	0.45	0.40	0.34	0.28	0.07
	0.21	0.14	0.08	0.02	-0.03	-0.08	-0.11	-0.14	-0.15	-0.15	-0.18	-0.19	0.23
Canada	0.97	0.92	0.87	0.82	0.77	0.73	0.68	0.64	0.60	0.56	0.53	0.50	0.07
	0.47	0.44	0.40	0.36	0.31	0.26	0.21	0.15	0.09	0.03	-0.02	-0.05	0.26
Switzerland	0.98	0.96	0.94	0.92	0.91	0.89	0.88	0.87	0.86	0.84	0.82	0.80	0.07
	0.78	0.76	0.73	0.71	0.69	0.67	0.65	0.64	0.62	0.60	0.58	0.56	0.30
United Kingdom	0.99	0.97	0.96	0.95	0.93	0.91	0.90	0.88	0.87	0.85	0.83	0.82	0.07
	0.81	0.79	0.78	0.76	0.75	0.73	0.72	0.70	0.69	0.67	0.75	0.64	0.31

NOTE: r_k represents an estimate of the kth order autocorrelation coefficient; s.e. is the estimated standard error for that row of the table.

TABLE 4

AUTOCORRELATIONS OF $\ln F_t$

(April 1973 - May 1977)

Country	r_1 / r_{13}	r_2 / r_{14}	r_3 / r_{15}	r_4 / r_{16}	r_5 / r_{17}	r_6 / r_{18}	r_7 / r_{19}	r_8 / r_{20}	r_9 / r_{21}	r_{10} / r_{22}	r_{11} / r_{23}	r_{12} / r_{24}	s.e.
Netherlands	0.96	0.91	0.85	0.79	0.73	0.68	0.63	0.58	0.54	0.49	0.45	0.40	0.07
	0.34	0.28	0.23	0.17	0.13	0.10	0.07	0.04	0.02	0.01	-0.01	-0.02	0.24
Germany	0.95	0.90	0.83	0.76	0.69	0.63	0.57	0.51	0.45	0.39	0.33	0.26	0.07
	0.19	0.12	0.06	-0.01	-0.06	-0.10	-0.13	-0.15	-0.17	-0.18	-0.19	-0.20	0.23
Canada	0.97	0.93	0.88	0.84	0.79	0.75	0.71	0.67	0.63	0.59	0.56	0.53	0.07
	0.50	0.47	0.43	0.39	0.34	0.29	0.23	0.17	0.12	0.06	0.02	-0.01	0.26
Switzerland	0.98	0.96	0.94	0.92	0.90	0.89	0.88	0.86	0.85	0.84	0.82	0.80	0.07
	0.77	0.75	0.73	0.71	0.69	0.67	0.65	0.63	0.62	0.60	0.58	0.56	0.30
United Kingdom	0.99	0.97	0.96	0.95	0.93	0.91	0.90	0.88	0.86	0.85	0.83	0.82	0.07
	0.80	0.79	0.77	0.76	0.74	0.73	0.71	0.70	0.68	0.66	0.65	0.63	0.31

NOTE: r_k represents an estimate of the kth order autocorrelation coefficient; s.e. is the standard error for that row of the table.

TABLE 5

AUTOCORRELATIONS OF $\ln S_t - \ln F_{t-4}$

(April 1973 – May 1977)

Country	r_1 / r_{13}	r_2 / r_{14}	r_3 / r_{15}	r_4 / r_{16}	r_5 / r_{17}	r_6 / r_{18}	r_7 / r_{19}	r_8 / r_{20}	r_9 / r_{21}	r_{10} / r_{22}	r_{11} / r_{23}	r_{12} / r_{24}	s.e.
Netherlands	0.85	0.65	0.40	0.17	0.02	-0.06	-0.08	-0.07	-0.02	0.03	0.06	0.06	0.07
	0.03	-0.02	-0.09	-0.14	-0.17	-0.18	-0.18	-0.18	-0.17	-0.16	-0.16	-0.18	0.14
Germany	0.85	0.65	0.42	0.22	0.08	0.02	0.00	-0.01	-0.01	-0.00	0.00	-0.03	0.07
	-0.07	-0.12	-0.19	-0.26	-0.30	-0.31	-0.30	-0.28	-0.23	-0.22	-0.22	-0.25	0.14
Canada	0.83	0.59	0.32	0.09	-0.02	-0.01	-0.01	0.04	0.07	-0.08	0.14	0.21	0.07
	0.28	0.35	0.38	0.36	0.29	0.15	0.05	-0.06	0.13	0.16	-0.15	-0.14	0.13
Switzerland	0.73	0.56	0.33	0.08	-0.03	-0.07	0.01	0.03	0.08	0.11	0.11	0.07	0.07
	0.03	-0.04	-0.12	-0.17	-0.20	-0.18	-0.14	-0.07	-0.05	-0.05	-0.10	-0.20	0.12
United Kingdom	0.87	0.71	0.54	0.38	0.28	0.22	0.13	0.06	0.01	-0.06	-0.10	-0.12	0.07
	-0.15	-0.15	-0.13	-0.10	-0.05	-0.02	-0.01	-0.02	-0.03	-0.06	-0.07	-0.09	0.15

NOTE: r_k represents an estimate of the kth order autocorrelation coefficient; s.e. is the estimated standard error for that row of the table.

CHAPTER II

FOREIGN EXCHANGE MARKET EFFICIENCY

2.1 Introduction

The hypothesis of efficiency has been used in many studies of the foreign exchange market. This hypothesis implies that there are no unexploited profit opportunities. In the foreign exchange market this implies that the forward rate summarizes all relevant and available information useful for forecasting the future spot rate. Analyzing this aspect of efficiency requires an equilibrium model of pricing in the foreign exchange market. Consequently, any empirical test of efficiency is a joint test of efficiency and the equilibrium model.

This chapter will focus on two different methods of testing market efficiency. Section 2.2 will examine the issue of efficiency from the point of view of the standard regression model. This procedure considers a regression of the spot rate on the lagged forward rate. Several econometric difficulties arise and must be overcome when the forecast horizon (one month) exceeds the sampling interval (one week). The stochastic structure of the error term can be interpreted as new information reaching the foreign exchange market. To analyze the nature of efficiency with this procedure requires an empirical analysis of the properties of the error term. This will be done in Section 2.3.

Section 2.4 will present a new, and alternative, procedure for analyzing the hypothesis of efficiency. This procedure is based on a time series

analysis of the spot and one month forward rate. It is assumed that the
spot and forward rate can be described as a bivariate stochastic process.
The structure of the stochastic process provides a convenient method for
extracting forecasts of the future spot rate as a function of all available
information (given the model being assumed). However, the hypothesis of
market efficiency states that, in general, the expected value of the future
spot rate is the current forward rate. We see, therefore, that the parameters of the original stochastic process are not free, but must be constrained. The restrictions are highly nonlinear. Section 2.4 will provide a computationally feasible method for calculating the likelihood function subject to these restrictions. The restrictions are then tested for
five currencies relative to the dollar. Section 2.5 concludes the chapter.

2.2 Econometric Testing and Procedures

Conventional tests of foreign exchange market efficiency focus on
the relation between spot and lagged forward rates. (Assume, for now, that
one month is exactly four weeks.) If one wants to forecast $\ln S_{t+4}$, based
on information up to (and including) time t, then the following regression
is appropriate:

$$\ln S_{t+4} = x_t' \beta + u_{t+4} \qquad (2.1)$$

where x_t represents variables relevant for forecasting $\ln S_{t+4}$, and where

$$E(u_{t+4} \colon \ln S_t, \ln S_{t-1}, \ldots, x_t, x_{t-1}, \ldots) = 0. \qquad (2.2)$$

Conditions (2.1) and (2.2) imply $E u_t u_{t-k} = 0$, for all $k \geq 4$, so that u_t is a
moving average of order 3 process, MA(3). The reason for this serial correlation of the errors is that the forecast horizon (four weeks) exceeds the
sampling interval (one week). This data overlapping problem induces serial

correlation since, loosely speaking, it takes four weeks to realize an error has been made. Appendix A discusses the implication of the fact that one month has approximately 4.3 weeks.

Given that u_t can be written as an MA(3) process, we can write $u_t = \varepsilon_t + \theta_1 \varepsilon_{t-1} + \theta_2 \varepsilon_{t-2} + \theta_3 \varepsilon_{t-3} = \theta(L)\varepsilon_t$. Notice that equation (2.2) does <u>not</u> require that x_t be strictly exogenous (at all leads and lags). Obtaining estimates of the β vector by ordinary least squares is equivalent to minimizing the sum of squared prediction errors. To test the forecasting ability of the forward rate, we shall restrict (2.1) by requiring x_t to consist of a constant and $\ln F_t$. That is, we shall consider the following regression:

$$\ln S_{t+4} = a + b \ln F_t + u_{t+4} \tag{2.1'}$$

where

$$E(u_{t+4} : \ln S_t, \ln S_{t-1}, \ldots, \ln F_t, \ln F_{t-1}, \ldots) = 0. \tag{2.2'}$$

For future reference let $I_t = \{\ln S_t, \ln S_{t-1}, \ldots, \ln F_t, \ln F_{t-1}, \ldots\}$. Restricting the x_t vector in this way will impose restrictions on the data that can be rejected. This restriction tests, basically, if the forward rate summarizes all information (and that the risk premium, if it exists, is such that equation (2.1') holds).

There are several difficulties involved in estimating equation (2.1') efficiently as a regression equation. The problem arises since $\ln F_t$ is not strictly exogenous (that is, $\ln F_t$ is a lagged endogenous variable) and the errors are serially correlated. The combination of these two facts causes problems for GLS estimation. As Maddala states, "Thus, when lagged endogenous variables are present, GLS estimators based on a consistent estimate of the covariance matrix are still consistent, but they do not

have the same limiting distribution as the estimates based on the true

value of the covariance matrix" (Maddala 1971, p. 25). However, as Sims

states, ". . . almost any of the slightly more sophisticated techniques in

common use (all those which reduce to or employ generalized least squares,

for example) require the stronger assumption that X_t is exogenous--i.e.,

that X_t and X_s are uncorrelated for all t and s" (Sims 1972, p. 17).

Hatanaka (1974) has proposed an efficient two-step estimator for a model

including a lagged dependent variable but with autoregressive errors. It

does not appear that there exists efficient two step GLS procedures with

lagged endogenous variables and MA error terms. It is, however, possible

to obtain consistent, but not fully efficient estimates of a and b by using

ordinary least squares.[1] It is not fully efficient since we do not use the

information that u_t is MA(3); it is, however, more efficient than dropping

three-fourths of the observations.

---

[1]The nature of the inconsistency in this case can be easily seen
(see Hansen 1979). Let u_t have an MA representation: $u_t = \theta(L)\varepsilon_t$, where
$\theta(L)$ is invertible, with inverse $\theta(L)^{-1}$. Multiplying equation (2.1') by
$\theta(L)^{-1}$ we have

$$\theta(L)^{-1}\ln S_{t+4} = a\theta(L)^{-1} + b\theta(L)^{-1}\ln F_t + \varepsilon_{t+4}.$$

Now, it is the case that ε_t is serially uncorrelated; however, in general
it will be the case that

$$E(\theta(L)^{-1}\ln S_{t+4} : \theta(1)^{-1}, \theta(L)^{-1}\ln F_t) \neq a\theta(1)^{-1} + b\theta(L)^{-1}\ln F_t$$

since we cannot rule out possible correlation between ε_{t+4} and $\theta(1)^{-1}\ln F_t$.

Hansen (1979) shows that the usual standard errors (as reported in
most computer packages) are incorrect. Under the assumption that $\{\ln S_t\}$
and $\{\ln F_t\}$ are stationary, and that the one-step ahead forecast errors are
constants, independent of I_{t-1}, the covariance matrix is $(X'X)^{-1}X'\hat{\Omega}X(X'X)^{-1}$,
where $\hat{\Omega}$ is the estimated variance-covariance matrix, with the zero restrictions imposed that $Eu_t u_{t-k} = 0$ for k > 6 (Hansen 1979).

A sufficient condition for the forward rate to be an unbiased forecast of the future spot rate is a = 0 and b = 1 in equation (2.1').[1] Two
of the studies using weekly data with a forward rate of maturity greater
than one week (Stockman 1978 used a one-month forward rate and Hansen and
Hodrick 1979 used a three month forward rate) constrained, a priori, b = 1.
Stockman set b = 1 so that he could estimate the moving average parameters
efficiently and Hansen and Hodrick set b = 1 to induce stationarity. However, in general, we know that constraining b = 1 may bias the other coefficient.[2]

Much of our interest in this chapter is focused on the residuals u_t.
There are two reasons for this. The first, discussed earlier, is that if
the forward rate is to be an efficient forecast of the future spot rate,
then the residuals should be a pure forecast error. The second reason
comes from considering the return from holding foreign currency. Let us
decompose the total return from holding foreign currency, $\ln S_{t+4} - \ln S_t$,
as follows:

$$\ln S_{t+4} - \ln S_t = (\ln S_{t+4} - E_t \ln S_{t+4}) + (E_t \ln S_{t+4} - \ln S_t) \qquad (2.3)$$

where we use the notation $E_t x_s = E(x_s : I_t)$.[3] Many studies look at the total

---

[1]If unbiasedness means $E(S_{t+4} : I_t) = F_t$ and u_t is normally distributed
in (3'), then it is easily shown that the "correct" null hypothesis is
$a = -\frac{1}{2} \sigma_u^2$ and b = 1 (see Frenkel 1979). A difficulty is that to state the
null hypothesis, one must make some distributional assumption on the residuals
(normally, we make distributional assumptions when we want to test the null
hypothesis (see Garber 1978).

[2]Consider a simple example (no serial correlation) where we project
(linearly) y_t on a constant x_0, x_{1t} and x_{2t}: $E(y_t : x_0, x_{1t}, x_{2t}) = b_0 + b_1 x_{1t} + b_2 x_{2t}$. Suppose we constrain b = 1, then $E(y_t - x_{1t} : x_0, x_{2t}) = a_0 + a_2 x_{2t}$. It can be shown that $b_2 = \text{cov}(x_{2t}, y_t)/\text{var}(x_{2t})$ and $a_2 = b_2 - \text{cov}(x_{2t}, x_{1t})/\text{var}(x_{2t})$.

[3]See Roll and Solnick (1977, p. 167) for a similar decomposition.

return (Poole 1967 and Bilson 1979). The second term on the right hand side, $E_t \ln S_{t+4} - \ln S_t$, is a known quantity (to the economic agent), it is the expected change as of time t in the exchange rate. The first term, $\ln S_{t+4} - E_t \ln S_{t+4}$, is a random variable that represents the unanticipated return from holding foreign currency, due to new information which affects the exchange rate. Since agents are compensated for bearing uncertainty, we are led to focus our attention on that term. But equation (2.1') states that $E_t \ln S_{t+4} = a + b \ln F_t$; hence $\ln S_{t+4} - E_t \ln S_{t+4} = u_{t+4}$.[1]

Equation (2.1') is only one possible regression that could be used to test the hypothesis of market efficiency. Appendix B examines the relative merits of using different functional forms.

We stated earlier that we could write $u_t = \theta(L)\varepsilon_t$, where $\theta(L)$ is a third degree polynomial in the lag operator L. We now want to provide an interpretation of the θ's. Since we can write $u_t = \theta(L)\varepsilon_t$, we can rewrite equation (2.1') as

$$\ln S_{t+4} = a + b \ln F_t + \theta_3 \varepsilon_{t+1} + \theta_2 \varepsilon_{t+2} + \theta_1 \varepsilon_{t+3} + \varepsilon_{t+4}. \qquad (2.1'')$$

Assuming the ε-shocks strike with equal weight over time, we see that we would expect the θ's to be approximately equal to 1. Appendix C derives an explicit formula relating θ_j^2 to the variance of the change in our forecast of u_{t+4}. The expression is

$$\theta_j = \left[\frac{Var(E_{t+4-j} u_{t+4} - E_{t+4-j-1} u_{t+4})}{Var(u_{t+4} - E_{t+3} u_{t+4})} \right]^{\frac{1}{2}}.$$

---

[1]Notice that equation (5) decomposes the total return into an expected return and an unexpected return term. To analyze the unexpected return, we are led to look at the residuals u_t from an equation of the log of S_{t+4} on the log of F_t.

2.3 Econometric Results

Equation (2.1') is estimated for five currencies with respect to the dollar.[1] Ordinary least squares estimates of a and b are reported in Table 6. In all cases b is less than one. However, only in the case of the Netherlands and Germany is b significantly less than one. In addition, the constant term is significantly less than zero for the Netherlands and Germany, but insignificantly different from zero for Canada, Switzerland and the U.K. These results indicate a significant risk premium for only the Netherlands and Germany.

Having obtained consistent estimates of a and b from Table 6, we can obtain a consistent estimate of u_t. An MA(4) process was fit to these OLS residuals. The results are reported in Table 6. θ_1 and θ_2 are generally within one standard deviation of unity and θ_3 is generally within two standard deviations of unity. Switzerland is the exception, where θ_1, θ_2, and θ_3 are all significantly less than 1.0. θ_4 is significantly less than 1.0, as expected, since ε_{t-4} is picking up "the last two days of the month." These results conform to our prior notion of the θ_j's.

As stated previously, b has often been constrained to be unity (Hansen and Hocrick 1979 and Stockman 1978). If b is in fact unity, then this method will provide efficient estimates of a. However, if the data rejects the assumption that b is unity, imposing this restriction will bias our results. Table 7 reports the estimates of a obtained from constraining b to be unity. We see that in all cases, a is insignificantly different from 0.[2]

---

[1] I wish to thank Alan C. Stockman for providing me with this data.

[2] Notice that this does not test a = 0 and b = 1. Table 4 provides an estimate of a given that b = 1.0. However, if we constrain b = 1 (incorrectly) then a is also biased; b is constrained to be larger than the data suggest and a is found to be smaller than the data suggest.

25

TABLE 6

$$\ln S_{t+4} = a + b \ln F_t + u_{t+4}$$

$$u_t \sim MA(4)$$

	Netherlands	Germany	Canada	Switzerland	United Kingdom
a	-0.230 (0.078)	-0.257 (0.075)	0.001 (0.000)	-0.084 (0.045)	0.013 (0.018)
b	0.757 (0.081)	0.719 (0.082)	0.915 (0.079)	0.913 (0.045)	0.979 (0.023)
θ_1	1.012 (0.064)	0.996 (0.064)	1.102 (0.056)	0.628 (0.069)	1.023 (0.067)
θ_2	1.076 (0.073)	0.964 (0.073)	1.070 (0.065)	0.682 (0.069)	0.939 (0.084)
θ_3	0.860 (0.071)	0.839 (0.070)	1.002 (0.064)	0.629 (0.068)	0.747 (0.083)
θ_4	0.378 (0.064)	0.441 (0.061)	0.629 (0.056)	0.226 (0.069)	0.336 (0.068)
σ_u^2	0.851	0.974	0.130	0.958	0.577
σ_ε^2	0.184	0.213	0.027	0.377	0.131
PER	0	0	0	0	0
Q(12)	10.7	7.4	13.8*	9.4	16.6*
Q(24)	23.7	20.1	30.0	19.0	30.8
Q(36)	30.9	30.7	34.0	41.5	34.4

NOTES: Standard errors are in parentheses. σ_u^2 and σ_ε^2 are in units of 10^{-3}. Both σ_u^2 and σ_ε^2 are calculated with back forecasting. PER gives the number of times (or the periods) that the actual cumulative periodogram exceeds the expected cumulative periodogram, at the 10 percent level of significance. Q(k) tests the null hypothesis that the first k autocorrelations are equal to zero. Q(k) is distributed as $\chi^2(k-q)$, where q is the number of parameters estimated. An asterisk (*) denotes significant at the 5 percent level of significance.

TABLE 7

$$\ln S_{t+4} = a + 1.0 \ln F_t + u_{t+4}$$

$$u_t \sim MA(4)$$

	Netherlands	Germany	Canada	Switzerland	United Kingdom
a	0.0036 (0.0044)	0.0024 (0.0048)	0.0007 (0.0018)	0.0024 (0.0044)	-0.0034 (0.0033)
θ_1	0.9883 (0.0660)	0.9821 (0.0648)	1.1029 (0.0549)	0.6239 (0.0698)	1.0264 (0.0675)
θ_2	1.0332 (0.0774)	0.9429 (0.0771)	1.0709 (0.0645)	0.6704 (0.0705)	0.9387 (0.0849)
θ_3	0.8017 (0.0759)	0.7870 (0.0752)	1.0055 (0.0630)	0.6099 (0.0697)	0.7466 (0.0839)
θ_4	0.3525 (0.0662)	0.4154 (0.0636)	0.6495 (0.0549)	0.2107 (0.0694)	0.3335 (0.0678)
σ_u^2	0.990	1.153	0.134	1.025	0.586
σ_ϵ^2	0.231	0.278	0.029	0.418	0.134
PER	0	0	0	0	0
Q(12)	6.8	3.5	14.3*	9.7	16.3*
Q(24)	21.1	19.7	30.6	20.0	31.2
Q(36)	32.7	32.1	34.7	43.8	35.6

NOTES: See notes to Table 6.

Estimates of θ_j are also reported in Table 7 for the case in which b is constrained to be unity. In this case, a and θ_j (j = 1, 2, 3. 4) are jointly estimated in an efficient manner; $\ln F_t$ was taken to the left hand side so that all right hand side variables (a constant) are strictly exogenous. The results are similar to those in Table 6, except that θ_3 is significantly different from unity for the Netherlands and Germany.

As stated previously, much of our interest is in the behavior of the residuals. In particular, does u_t follow an MA(4) process, or equivalently, is ε_t white noise? To test this, a number of tests of ε_t being white noise are reported. Durbin's periodogram test (Durbin 1969) provides a frequency domain test of the null hypothesis that ε_t is white noise, against the alternative hypothesis that ε_t is not white noise (PER in the tables). PER = 0 means that the actual cumulative periodogram does not differ significantly from the expected cumulative periodogram, at any frequency. The Box-Pierce Q-statistic, Q(k), tests the null hypothesis that the first k autocorrelations are equal to zero. It can be shown that Q(k) is distributed as $\chi^2(k-q)$, where q is the number of parameters estimated. Related to the Box-Pierce Q-statistic, we can calculate the autocorrelation function of ε_t. So far, we have considered a very broad alternative: ε_t is not white noise. It is possible to test more restrictive alternative hypotheses.[1] One particular alternative that is considered is that u_t is MA(5).

The results of these tests of white noise are reported in Table 6. In all cases, Durbin's periodogram test indicates that ε_t is white noise (PER = 0 in the table). The Box-Pierce Q-statistic also indicates that ε_t is white noise for the Netherlands, Germany and Switzerland. However, for Canada and the U.K., the Box-Pierce Q(12) statistic of 13.8 and 16.6 indicate that there is a departure from white noise, at the 5 percent level of significance for these currencies. (Note that Q(12) is insignificant at the

---

[1]The power of a test relates to the alternative hypothesis. A test may be powerful against some alternatives but less powerful against other alternatives. Durbin's periodogram test has good power against the alternative of white noise, however, there are more powerful tests against, for example, an MA(1) alternative.

1 percent level and Q(24) and Q(36) are insignificant at the 5 percent level.)

Table 8 reports the first twelve autocorrelations of ε_t. In no case is any individual autocorrelation coefficient greater than two standard deviations from the null hypothesis of zero. However, r_2, r_4, r_7, r_9 and r_{10} for Canada, are individually greater than one standard deviation; $r_2 - r_6$ and $r_9 - r_{12}$, for the U.K., are also individually greater than one standard deviation.

To test if u_t is MA(5), we fit an MA(5) process to the OLS residuals. The results are reported in Table 9. We find that θ_5 is statistically significant for all currencies except Canada and the U.K. This would seem to imply that although for these currencies there is serial correlation in u_t beyond an MA(4), it is not of a moving average form. To test this assertion, one can perform a likelihood ratio test of whether one needs to go to an MA(5) process for u_t (over an MA(4)). The results of this test are reported in Table 10 under the column headed "Error." For the Netherlands and Switzerland, we see that going to an MA(5) yields significantly better results at the 10 percent level, but not significantly better at the 5 percent level, as indicated by χ^2 values of 3.32 and 3.79, respectively. For Germany, Canada and the U.K. there is no significant improvement at the 10 percent level. In fact, for Canada and the U.K., the variance of ε_t is unchanged, reflected in χ^2 values of 0.000, thereby confirming our earlier assertion. The results for the Netherlands and Switzerland tend to confirm Mussa's observation (Mussa 1979, p. 5) that "changes in exchange rates are not serially uncorrelated, but tend to follow a moving average process," where the moving average parameter is quite small. Given that θ_5 is quite small (relative to the other θ's), we may say that u_t is "approximately" MA(4), and that the

TABLE 8

AUTOCORRELATION FUNCTION FOR ε_{t+4}

$$\ln S_{t+4} = a + b\ln F_t + u_{t+4}$$
$$u_{t+4} = \Theta(L)\varepsilon_{t+4}$$

(April 1973 – May 1977)

	Netherlands	Germany	Canada	Switzerland	United Kingdom
r_1	0.01	0.02	-0.02	0.03	0.03
r_2	0.05	0.07	0.07	0.06	0.09
r_3	0.10	0.06	0.03	0.01	0.12
r_4	0.12	0.09	-0.10	0.01	0.10
r_5	0.05	0.08	0.06	0.02	0.12
r_6	-0.12	-0.04	0.05	-0.14	0.07
r_7	0.03	0.03	-0.11	0.09	-0.00
r_8	0.02	0.08	0.06	-0.02	0.01
r_9	0.07	0.03	0.12	0.09	0.09
r_{10}	0.01	0.02	-0.10	0.06	-0.10
r_{11}	0.04	0.06	0.06	0.04	-0.07
r_{12}	0.02	-0.03	0.03	-0.02	0.09

NOTES: r_k is the estimate of the Kth order autocorrelation coefficient. The standard error is 0.07.

TABLE 9

$$\ln S_{t+4} = a + b\ln F_t + u_{t+4}$$
$$u_t \sim MA(5)$$

	Netherlands	Germany	Canada	Switzerland	United Kingdom
a	-0.230 (0.078)	-0.257 (0.075)	0.001 (0.000)	-0.084 (0.045)	0.013 (0.018)
b	0.757 (0.081)	0.719 (0.082)	0.915 (0.079)	0.913 (0.045)	0.979 (0.023)
θ_1	0.999 (0.068)	1.009 (0.070)	1.100 (0.071)	0.677 (0.070)	1.033 (0.071)
θ_2	1.050 (0.088)	1.008 (0.091)	1.067 (0.095)	0.773 (0.080)	0.974 (0.097)
θ_3	0.928 (0.093)	0.912 (0.095)	0.996 (0.098)	0.778 (0.080)	0.819 (0.103)
θ_4	0.578 (0.086)	0.547 (0.089)	0.620 (0.096)	0.364 (0.080)	0.422 (0.097)
θ_5	0.222 (0.065)	0.122 (0.066)	0.006 (0.069)	0.171 (0.067)	0.086 (0.069)
σ_u^2	0.851	0.974	0.130	0.958	0.577
σ_ε^2	0.181	0.212	0.027	0.370	0.131
PER	0	0	0	0	0
Q(12)	3.8	4.4	13.7	5.5	14.2*
Q(24)	15.3	15.0	30.1	13.3	28.0
Q(36)	24.7	26.9	34.1	35.9	31.5

NOTE: See notes to Table 6.

TABLE 10

HYPOTHESIS TESTING RESULTS

Country	Error	Variance	Theta
Netherlands	3.32	4.31	12.81
Germany	0.95	3.94	5.00
Canada	0.00	0.53	16.27
Switzerland	3.79	6.90	6.89
United Kingdom	0.00	0.58	4.53

NOTE: The column Error tests the hypothesis that u_t is MA(4) against MA(5). A likelihood ratio test is used, where $2\ln\lambda$ is distributed $\chi^2(1)$, where

where $\lambda = \left[\dfrac{\sigma_2^2(MA4)}{\sigma_\varepsilon^2(MA5)} \right]^{(T/2)}$. The critical values are 2.71 (10 percent),

3.84 (5 percent) and 6.63 (1 percent). The column Variance tests the hypothesis that the variance of ε_t is equal in both periods ($\sigma^2(PER1) = \sigma^2(PER2)$) against the hypothesis that they are unequal. An F-statistic is calculated as $F = s_1^2/s_2^2$, F is distributed as F(99,97). Critical values, using F(100,100), for the two sided alternative are: $0.719 < F < 1.39$ (10 percent) and $0.629 < F < 1.59$ (2 percent). To test if the variance decreases over time, the critical values are 1.39 (5 percent) and 1.59 (1 percent). To test if the variance increases over time, the critical values are 0.719 (5 percent) and 0.629 (1 percent). The column Theta tests the hypothesis that $\theta(PER) = \theta(PER2)$. A χ^2 statistic can be calculated to test this hypothesis (see Morrison 1967). The critical values for $\chi^2(4)$ are 7.78 (10 percent), 9.49 (5 percent) and 13.3 (1 percent).

forecast error follows "approximately" a pure forecast error.

In equation (2.3) we decomposed the total return into an expected and unexpected return, and argued that we were interested in the unexpected return, $\ln S_{t+4} - E_t \ln S_t = \ln S_{t+4} - a - b\ln F_t$. For comparison with these other studies, we present in Table 11 the result of fitting a moving average process to the total return, $\ln S_{t+4} - \ln S_t$. As argued in Appendix A,

TABLE 11

$$\ln S_{t+4} = a + 1.0 \ln S_t + u_{t+4}$$

$$u_t \sim MA(3)$$

	Netherlands	Germany	Canada	Switzerland	United Kingdom
a	0.0068 (0.0009)	0.0035 (0.0032)	-0.0015 (0.0012)	0.0048 (0.0029)	-0.0066 (0.0008)
θ_1	1.0745 (0.0178)	0.9906 (0.0111)	1.0370 (0.0110)	0.9898 (0.0120)	1.0084 (0.0071)
θ_2	1.1015 (0.0036)	0.9935 (0.0107)	1.0154 (0.0151)	0.9567 (0.0219)	0.9861 (0.0118)
θ_3	0.9993 (0.0064)	0.9928 (0.0093)	0.9815 (0.0126)	0.9760 (0.0131)	0.9963 (0.0081)
σ_u^2	0.995	1.159	0.134	1.030	0.589
σ_ε^2	0.136	0.179	0.023	0.220	0.112
PER	7.5-10.6	5.3, 5.5, 6.3- 7.2, 9.2-10.6	5.6-8.4	0	0
Q(12)	19.9*	13.1	12.1	8.2	15.8
Q(24)	34.7*	32.1*	31.7*	16.9	35.8*
Q(36)	43.8	51.8*	35.7	42.2	41.8

NOTES: See notes to Table 6.

$\ln S_{t+4} - \ln S_t$ is predicted to follow an MA(3) process. We notice that the
constant is significantly positive for the Netherlands and significantly
negative for the U.K. The θ's are all individually insignificantly different unity, except for θ_1 for Canada. However, in looking at the periodogram test and the Q statistics, we find that, except for Switzerland, the
residuals do not behave like white noise. For the Netherlands, Germany

and Canada, the periodogram indicates significant cycles in the residuals
with a period of close to seven weeks (from a low of 5.3 weeks for Germany
to a high of 10.6 weeks for the Netherlands and Germany). What this sug-
gests, taken in conjunction with Tables 6, 7 and 9, is that in forecasting
the future spot rate, the current forward rate is more efficient than the
current spot rate.

As stated earlier, another issue of interest concerns the behavior
of the system over time. For example, can we assert in any meaningful
way that the system has become less noisy over time? Also, have economic
agents reacted to new information in the same way over time? To answer
these questions, we have divided the sample period into two equal halves
(non-overlapping) and reestimated equation (2.1') for each half. The results are presented in Tables 12 (first period, PER1) and 13 (second period,
PER2). An F-statistic can be calculated to test the hypothesis that σ_ε^2 is
the same in both periods. The results of such a calculation are reported
in Table 10 under the column headed "Variance." In all cases we can reject
the hypothesis (at the 10 percent and 2 percent level) that the variances
are equal, due to the extreme values of the F reported. For the Netherlands,
Germany and Switzerland we can accept the alternative (at the 5 percent and
1 percent level) that the variance has increased over time, as reflected in
the large values of F. On the other hand, for Canada and the U.K., we can
accept the alternative (at the 5 percent and 1 percent level) that the
variance has increased over time, as reflected in the small values of F.

The reaction of economic agents to the new information hitting the
market is summarized by the θ-vector. A χ^2 test can be used to test if the
θ's change over time. The result of such a test is reported in Table 10
under the column headed "Theta." For the Netherlands and Canada, one can

TABLE 12

$$\ln S_{t+4} = a + b \ln F_t + u_{t+4}$$

$$u_t \sim MA(4)$$

(April 1973 – April 1975)

	Netherlands	Germany	Canada	Switzerland	United Kingdom
a	-0.231	-0.298	-0.001	-0.096	0.301
b	0.765	0.672	0.972	0.904	0.652
θ_1	0.972 (0.093)	0.988 (0.090)	0.978 (0.093)	0.506 (0.091)	0.981 (0.097)
θ_2	1.017 (0.106)	0.924 (0.103)	0.906 (0.101)	0.660 (0.063)	0.849 (0.110)
θ_3	0.799 (0.102)	0.827 (0.098)	0.847 (0.097)	0.835 (0.050)	0.831 (0.109)
θ_4	0.341 (0.093)	0.459 (0.086)	0.402 (0.090)	0.430 (0.086)	0.414 (0.096)
σ_u^2	1.211	1.473	0.067	1.583	0.352
σ_ε^2	0.302	0.339	0.018	0.642	0.083
PER	0	0	0	0	0
Q(12)	5.1	4.3	12.6	9.8	9.3
Q(24)	15.7	16.1	24.2	18.8	20.3
Q(36)	22.0	23.4	32.5	37.4	25.4

NOTES: See notes to Table 6.

TABLE 13

$$\ln S_{t+4} = a + b\ln F_t + u_{t+4}$$

$$u_t \sim MA(4)$$

(May 1975 - May 1977)

	Netherlands	Germany	Canada	Switzerland	United Kingdom
a	-0.259	-0.192	0.002	-0.170	0.069
b	0.730	0.792	0.919	0.820	0.879
θ_1	1.140 (0.083)	1.056 (0.093)	1.232 (0.067)	0.866 (0.098)	1.010 (0.098)
θ_2	1.269 (0.077)	1.121 (0.102)	1.283 (0.064)	0.950 (0.101)	0.930 (0.121)
θ_3	1.177 (0.065)	0.942 (0.099)	1.230 (0.045)	0.836 (0.099)	0.715 (0.119)
θ_4	0.598 (0.078)	0.414 (0.091)	0.782 (0.060)	0.282 (0.098)	0.313 (0.097)
σ_u^2	0.487	0.451	0.194	0.325	0.495
σ_ε^2	0.070	0.086	0.034	0.093	0.142
PER	0	0	0	0	0
Q(12)	20.3*	10.1	8.5	10.1	8.5
Q(24)	26.0	17.1	15.9	18.2	23.3
Q(36)	29.2	19.8	22.1	24.9	28.2

NOTES: See notes to Table 6.

reject, at the 5 percent level, the hypothesis that the θ's are the same
in both periods. For Germany, Switzerland and the U.K. we cannot reject
the hypothesis that the θ's are the same in both periods. As a general
proposition, it appears that θ(period 2) is larger than θ(period 1).

To try and summarize the results in Tables 6-13, let us see what
patterns appear to emerge. In examining the behavior of the θ-vector in
Tables 6 and 7, we see that for Germany and Switzerland the θ's are less
than one (though not always significantly), and for Canada the θ's are
(insignificantly) greater than one. In addition, there is a general tendency
(though not exact) for the θ's to decrease in size. Finally, for Switzerland,
the θ's in Tables 6, 7, 9 and 12 are significantly less than one, approximately 0.7. However, in Table 11 where we look at the total return, the
θ's are insignificantly different from one. Therefore, although the θ-vectors
are generally insignificantly different from one, taken as a whole, certain
country specific patterns appear to hold. This of course is only an approxi-
mate statement since the five exchange rates are not independent. Finally,
although the slope is significantly less than one only for the Netherlands
and Germany, the point estimates are always less than one. Again, this is
not an exact statement since the five exchange rates are not independent.
What these last two facts suggest is that pooling all five countries might
lead to more precise estimates. In fact, this is what Bilson (1979) finds
in a slightly different context.

In addition, we see that it is possible to divide the sample into
two groups: (1) Canada and the U.K. and (2) the Netherlands, Germany and
Switzerland. For Canada and the U.K., the constant in equation (2.1') is
negative, while for the others it is positive. For a given slope, this
means that with respect to the Canadian dollar and U.K. pound, the dollar

is safer. For the other countries, the positive constants indicate that the dollar is riskier. Canada and the U.K. were the only countries that showed any sign of serial correlation in the ε_t (Q(12) was significant at the 5 percent level). This indicates that for these two countries, $\ln F_t$ did not summarize all information about the value of $\ln S_{t+4}$. (It should be noted that all other tests of randomness indicated lack of serial correlation in ε_t.) Finally, σ_ε^2 increased in the second period for Canada and the U.K., while it decreased for the others. How, then, is Canada and the U.K. different from the Netherlands, Germany and Switzerland?

From Tables 1 and 2, we see that the U.S. dollar appreciated against the Canadian dollar and U.K. pound for the period as a whole, while it depreciated against the other currencies. Not coincidently, Canada and the U.K. had the highest rates of inflation for the whole period and each of the two subperiods.

To understand the change in the variance of the system (σ_ε^2) we should consider some of the institutional details. In March of 1973, Germany and the Netherlands agreed to fix their rates within 2.5 percent but to float against the dollar. Late 1973 witnessed the dramatic increase in the price of oil. In December 1975 (at the Rambouillet meeting) and January 1976 (in Jamaica) it became "official" that we were in a period of floating exchange rates; previously, there was some hope of a return to fixed exchange rates. Finally, in late 1976 we have the IMF support of the sterling: in June of 1976, a $5 billion stand-by credit and in December of 1976, a $3.9 billion loan.

2.4 A New Procedure

In equation (2.1') we wrote $E(\ln S_{t+4}: I_t) = a + b \ln F_t$. This is quite a strong assumption and we would like some way to test it. One

possibility is to include variables x_{it} in the regression equation (2.1')
and test if the coefficients are significant (see, for example, Hansen and
Hodrick 1979); we would like a more efficient method. In addition, we
would like to obtain a more efficient estimate of b. We now turn to these
matters.

Assume $\{s_t, f_t\}$ is a bivariate, linearly indeterministic, covariance-
stationary stochastic process (see Sargent 1979b, for a good exposition of
the general methodology).[1] We will assume in the empirical work, that s_t
and f_t are the first differences of the logs of S_t and F_t. The Wold decomposition theorem allows us to express $\{s_t, f_t\}$ as an (infinite) order
bivariate moving average process:

$$s_t = \alpha(L)w_t + \beta(L)v_t$$

$$f_t = \gamma(L)w_t + \delta(L)v_t$$

(2.4)

where $\alpha(L)$, $\beta(L)$, $\gamma(L)$ and $\delta(L)$ are one-sided polynomials in the lag
operator L,

$$w_t = s_t - E(s_t: s_{t-1}, s_{t-2}, \ldots, f_{t-1}, f_{t-2}, \ldots)$$

$$v_t = f_t - E(f_t: s_{t-1}, s_{t-2}, \ldots, f_{t-1}, f_{t-2}, \ldots)$$

$$Ew_t w_{t-k} = \begin{cases} \sigma_w^2 & k = 0 \\ 0 & k \neq 0 \end{cases}$$

$$Ev_t v_{t-k} = \begin{cases} \sigma_v^2 & k = 0 \\ 0 & k \neq 0 \end{cases}$$

---

[1]This implies that the variances of s_t and f_t exist and are independent of t, the covariance between s_t and f_{t-s} exist and are functions
of s alone, and the means of s_t and f_t are zero.

$$Ew_t v_{t-k} = \begin{cases} \sigma_{wv} & k = 0 \\ 0 & k \neq 0 \end{cases}$$

$\alpha(0) = \delta(0) = 1$ and $\beta(0) = \gamma(0) = 0$.

Using the Weiner-Kolmogorov prediction formulas, we obtain

$$E_t s_{t+4} = \left[\frac{(L)}{L^4}\right]_+ w_t + \left[\frac{(L)}{L^4}\right]_+ v_t \tag{2.5}$$

where $[\ ]_+$ means "ignore negative powers of L."

Imposing the condition that $E_t \ln S_{t+4} = a + b \ln F_t$ is equivalent to $E_t s_{t+4} = bf_t$. Combining this with equation (2.4) yields

$$E_t s_{t+4} = b\gamma(L)w_t + b\delta(L)v_t. \tag{2.6}$$

Equating equations (2.5) and (2.6) we obtain the following cross-equation restrictions on the parameters of the Wold Representation:[1]

$$b\gamma(L) = \left[\frac{\alpha(L)}{L^4}\right]_+$$
$$\tag{2.7}$$
$$b\delta(L) = \left[\frac{\beta(L)}{L^4}\right]_+$$

These restrictions provide the content of the theory and are refutable.

We can now test the hypothesis that f_t summarizes all information.[2] Assume we can truncate the infinite sums in (2.4) at lag M. One can then

---

[1]These restrictions can also be written as $b\gamma_0 = \alpha_4$, $b\gamma_1 = \alpha_5$, ..., $b\delta_0 = \beta_4$, $b\delta_1 = \beta_5$, ...

[2]"Summarizes all information" is being used in the restricted sense of summarizing the entire past history of s_t and f_t.

calculate the unconstrained and constrained likelihood functions and calculate a likelihood ratio statistic. Under the additional assumption that
$\ln F_t$ is an unbiased forecast of $\ln S_{t+4}$, we obtain a new set of cross-
equation restrictions, obtained by setting $b=1$ in equation (2.7). One
can then test this hypothesis using a likelihood ratio statistic.

Given that we wish to impose the assumption that f_t summarizes all
information (that is, equation (2.1') is correct), we can interpret the θ's
of equation (2.1"). Appendix C shows that the θ's and σ_ε^2 can be solved for
as highly nonlinear functions of the underlying parameters: $\{\alpha_0, \alpha_1, \alpha_2,$
$\alpha_3, \beta_0, \beta_1, \beta_2, \beta_3, \sigma_w^2, \sigma_v^2, \sigma_{wv}\}$.

To summarize, we see that $z_{t+4} = s_{t+4} - E_t s_{t+4}$ can be written as
an MA(3) process, $\theta(L)\varepsilon_{t+4}$. ε_{t+4} is a linear combination of the entire
past history of one-step ahead forecasts, and therefore, of the entire
past history of $\{s_t, f_t\}$. The weights θ_j are highly nonlinear functions of
the $\alpha_i, \beta_j, \sigma_w^2, \sigma_v^2$ and σ_{wv}.

The difficulty in this test procedure is due to the inability to
estimate constrained vector moving averages (at the University of Chicago).
Under the assumption that $\{s_t, f_t\}$ is invertible, we can estimate a bivariate autoregression for $\{s_t, f_t\}$ (the α, β, γ and δ polynomials are
different from those in equation (2.4), however, w_t and v_t are the same as
in equation (2.4)):

$$s_t = \sum_{i=1}^{M} \alpha_i s_{t-i} + \sum_{i=1}^{M} \beta_i f_{t-1} + w_t \qquad (2.8a)$$

$$f_t = \sum_{i=1}^{M} \gamma_i s_{t-1} + \sum_{i=1}^{M} \delta_i f_{t-1} + v_t. \qquad (2.8b)$$

To estimate $(\alpha, \beta, \gamma, \delta)$ let us rewrite (2.8) as a first order vector stochastic difference equation. Define the matrix A, and vectors x_t and a_t as

41

$$A = \begin{bmatrix} \alpha_1 & \alpha_2 & \cdots & \alpha_M & \beta_1 & \beta_2 & \cdots & \beta_M \\ 1 & 0 & & 0 & 0 & 0 & & 0 \\ 0 & 1 & & 0 & 0 & 0 & & 0 \\ 0 & 0 & & 1 & 0 & 0 & 0 & 0 \\ \gamma_1 & \gamma_2 & \cdots & \gamma_M & \delta_1 & \delta_2 & & \delta_M \\ 0 & 0 & & 0 & 1 & 0 & & 0 \\ \vdots & & & & & & & \\ 0 & 0 & & 0 & 0 & 0 & & 1 & 0 \end{bmatrix} \quad \leftarrow \text{row } M+1$$

$$X_t = \begin{bmatrix} s_t \\ s_{t-1} \\ \vdots \\ s_{t-M+1} \\ f_t \\ f_{t-1} \\ \vdots \\ f_{t-M+1} \end{bmatrix} \qquad a_t = \begin{bmatrix} w_t \\ 0 \\ \vdots \\ 0 \\ v_t \\ 0 \\ \vdots \\ 0 \end{bmatrix} \quad \leftarrow \text{row } M+1.$$

Then, we can rewrite equation (2.8) as

$$x_t = A\,x_{t-1} + a_t. \tag{2.9}$$

Defining $c = (1\ 0\ \ldots\ 0)$ and $d = (0\ \ldots\ 0\ 1\ 0\ \ldots\ 0)$, we can rewrite (2.8), using (2.9), as

$$s_t = c \, A \, x_{t-1} + w_t$$

$$f_t = d \, A \, x_{t-1} + v_t. \tag{2.10}$$

Update equation (2.9) by $+ j$ to get

$$
\begin{aligned}
x_{t+j} &= A \, x_{t+j-1} + a_{t+j} \\
&= A[A \, x_{t+j-2} + a_{t+j-1}] + a_{t+j} \\
&\quad \cdot \\
&\quad \cdot \\
&\quad \cdot \\
&= A^{j+1} \, x_{t-1} + A^{j} \, a_t + \ldots + a_{t+j}.
\end{aligned}
\tag{2.11}
$$

Taking expectations of both sides of (2.11), conditional on information up to $t - 1$, I_{t-1}, we get

$$E(x_{t+j} | I_{t-1}) = A^{j+1} \, x_{t-1}. \tag{2.12}$$

Recalling that $s_t = c \, A \, x_{t-1} + w_t$, we can calculate $E_{t-1} s_t$ by pre-multiplying both sides of (2.12) by the (row) vector c:

$$E_{t-1} \, s_{t+j} = E(c \, x_{t+j} | I_{t-1}) = c \, A^{j+1} \, x_{t-1}. \tag{2.13}$$

The assumption that f_t summarizes all information implies that

$$E(s_{t+4} | I_{t-1} = b \, E(f_t | I_{t-1}).$$

From (2.10) we have that

$$b \, E(f_t | I_{t-1}) = b(dA) \, x_{t-1}. \tag{2.14}$$

Therefore, by equating equations (2.13) and (2.14), we obtain the following set of cross-equation restrictions:

$$b(dA) = c \, A^5. \tag{2.15}$$

Equation (2.15) is analogous to equation (2.7). Under the further assumption that the forward rate is an unbiased estimate of the future spot rate, we have that b = 1. Therefore, the restrictions embodied in (2.15) become

$$dA = cA^5. \tag{2.16}$$

Under the hypothesis that $\{w_t, v_t\}$ is bivariate normal, the likelihood function of a sample of size T of $\{w_t, v_t\}$ can be written

$$L(\alpha, \beta, \gamma, \delta \mid \{s_t\}, \{f_t\}) = (2\pi)^{-T} |V|^{-T/2} \exp\{-1/2 \sum_{t=1}^{T} e_t' V^{-1} e_t\} \tag{2.17}$$

where

$$e_t = \begin{bmatrix} w_t \\ \\ v_t \end{bmatrix} \qquad V = E\, e_t e_t'.$$

Maximizing (2.17) unconstrained is equivalent to estimating (2.8) by least squares (to obtain efficient standard errors, one would use Zellner's unrelated regression).

The restrictions implied by equations (2.15) and (2.16) are highly nonlinear. First, let us consider two estimation strategies for the restriction implied by b = 1, namely equation (2.16). Sargent (1979b) proposes two alternative estimation strategies. The first method requires estimating the first row of A, equation (2.8a), by least squares. Then, the (M+1) st row of A, equation (2.8b), is calculated using an iterative procedure. Form a preliminary estimate of A, call it A_o, by setting row M + 1 to a row of zeroes, and all other rows to their known (or consistent) values. Calculate the (M+1)st row of A, at iteration i + 1, as

$$(\text{row M+1})_{i+1} = dA_{i+1} = c\, A_i^5 \tag{2.18}$$

where A_i is the estimate of A on the i'th iteration. At each step in form-
ing A_i, all rows (except the (M+1)st) are kept equal to the corresponding
row of A_o. If this procedure converges, it will find an A that satisfies
(2.16). Since the elements of row 1 are consistently estimated by least
squares, the (M+1)st row will be consistently estimated as a function of
the first row of A.

Define the solution to the iteration on (2.18) as the (set) function

$$(\gamma, \delta) = \phi(\alpha, \beta) \tag{2.19}$$

ϕ maps the α's and β's into a set of γ's and δ's that satisfy restriction
(2.16). Hence, one (consistent) estimator of γ, δ is $\phi(\alpha, \beta)$. (Call this
the "Two Step Estimator.")

To estimate equation (2.8), with restriction (2.15) imposed is
analogous. As before, we begin by estimating the first row of A, equation
(2.8a), by least squares. An initial guess for b is obtained from Table 6.
Then, the (M+1)st row of A, equation (2.8b), is calculated using an iterative procedure. In a manner similar to before, we can obtain as a solution
to the iteration procedure the set function $\tilde{\phi}$, $\tilde{\phi}(\alpha, \beta, b) = (\gamma, \delta)$. $\tilde{\phi}$ maps
the α's, β's and b into a set of γ's and δ's that satisfy restriction (2.15).

Under the restriction (2.16) (equivalently (2.19)), the likelihood
function in (2.17), $L(\alpha, \beta, \gamma, \sigma/\{s_t\}, \{f_t\})$, becomes a function only of
the α's and β's. As Wilson (1973) argues, maximum likelihood estimates with
an unknown V are obtained by minimizing $|\hat{V}|$, with respect to the α's and β's,
where

$$|\hat{V}| = \left| \frac{1}{T} \sum_{t=1}^{T} e_t(\alpha, \beta) \, e_t(\alpha, \beta)' \right|$$

where the $e_t(\alpha, \beta)$, the residuals from (2.8), are functions of the α's and β's only, since they were calculated from (2.8) with (2.16) (equivalently (2.19)) imposed.

A derivative free nonlinear minimization routine can be used to estimate (2.8) under the restriction (2.16) or (2.15). The IMSL subroutine ZXMIN, which uses a quasi-Newton method, was used. Generally, 600 iterations (at a cost of \$45) were required to obtain three significant digits. The least squares estimates of α and β were used as starting values.

A possible criticism of our previous approach is that the estimates of a and b are biased, due to left out variables. For example, it might be argued that the level of the balance of payments is important and belongs in equation (2.3'). The approach we have just outlined is not subject to such a criticism. Let Ω_t represent <u>all</u> information available at time t, including at least the past history of S_t and F_t, call it I_t. The hypothesis is that

$$F_t = E(S_{t+4} : \Omega_t). \qquad (2.20)$$

A correct way to test this is to run S_{t+4} against F_t and all other variables belonging in Ω_t and test if all the coefficients are unity and all zeroes. This requires knowing, a priori, all variables that belong in Ω_t. Alternatively, project linearly, both sides of (2.20) against I_t, to get

$$E(F_t : I_t) = E[E(S_{t+4} : \Omega) : I_t].$$

Noticing that $E(F_t : I_t) = F_t$ and using the law of iterated projections we can simplify the above expression to

$$F_t = E(S_{t+4} : F_t, F_{t-1}, \ldots, S_t, S_{t-1}, \ldots)$$

which is just expression (2.1') and (2.2') used previously.

Tables 14-18 report three estimates of equation (2.8) under various assumptions for the five currencies vis-à-vis the U.S. dollar. The tables report estimates of the bivariate autoregression (2.8) unconstrained, the maximum likelihood estimates that impose (2.16) (b=1) and the maximum likelihood estimates that impose (2.15) (b free). Also re-reported are the row sums of the α's, β's, γ's and δ's. The likelihood ratio statistic, which is distributed $\chi^2(8)$, and the marginal significance level, which is the probability that a random variable that is distributed $\chi^2(8)$ attains a value greater than or equal to the test statistic, are also reported.

According to the likelihood ratio statistic, the hypothesis is generally rejected. Only for Germany, with b free, is the marginal significance level greater than 0.02. A vector stochastic process is said to be stationary if the roots of a certain determinantal equation are all less than one in absolute value (see Whittle 1963, p. 29). Such was found to be the case for all currencies.

There appears to be a number of regularities that can be found in these results, some of which may be related to the cause for rejection. One regularity concerns the sign pattern of the coefficients. In all cases but two (Canada and the U.K.), the sum of the α_i's and the sum of the δ_i's are negative, while the sum of the β_i's and the sum of the γ_i's are positive. Recall that the α's are the coefficients on lagged s_t's and the β's are the coefficients on lagged f_t's in the s_t equation, while the γ's are the coefficients on lagged s_t's and the δ's are the coefficients on lagged f_t's in the f_t equation. In other words, the "own" lagged coefficients are negative while the "cross" lagged coefficients are positive. This indicates that if s_t is high this period, s will be lower next period and

TABLE 14

NETHERLANDS: ESTIMATES OF BIVARIATE AUTOREGRESSION
UNRESTRICTED AND RESTRICTED

j	1	2	3	4	Row Sum
		Unrestricted Estimates			
α_j	0.01913	-0.04513	-0.01726	-0.00722	-0.05049
β_j	0.26103	0.08057	0.06862	-0.02894	0.38128
γ_j	0.82962	0.49743	0.20908	0.00174	1.53787
δ_j	-0.51371	-0.35106	-0.14112	0.01910	-0.98679

$$\hat{V} = \begin{pmatrix} 1.303*10^{-4} & 8.345*10^{-5} \\ & 9.713*10^{-5} \end{pmatrix} \quad |\hat{V}| = 5.692*10^{-9}$$

Maximum Likelihood Estimates
b=1

j	1	2	3	4	Row Sum
α_j	-0.56550	-0.59600	-0.40654	-0.40114	-1.96918
β_j	0.68043	0.56195	0.44296	0.16306	1.84840
γ_j	0.29193	0.07700	0.02809	0.04198	0.43900
δ_j	-0.17457	-0.05475	-0.04048	-0.01706	-0.25686

$$\hat{V} = \begin{pmatrix} 1.541*10^{-4} & 1.061*10^{-5} \\ & 1.159*10^{-4} \end{pmatrix} \quad |\hat{V}| = 6.596*10^{-9}$$

Likelihood ratio statistic = 29.775
Marginal significance level = 0.00023

Maximum Likelihood Estimates
b free

j	1	2	3	4	Row Sum
α_j	-0.65142	-0.65475	-0.29087	-0.18303	-1.78007
β_j	0.82390	0.55780	0.25424	0.03786	1.67380
γ_j	0.32057	0.10130	0.01639	0.06781	0.50607
δ_j	-0.11494	-0.08055	-0.07529	-0.01403	-0.28481

b = 0.44848

$$\hat{V} = \begin{pmatrix} 1.577*10^{-4} & 1.054*10^{-4} \\ & 1.116*10^{-4} \end{pmatrix} \quad |\hat{V}| = 6.492*10^{-9}$$

Likelihood ratio statistic = 26.503
Marginal significance level = 0.00086

TABLE 15

GERMANY: ESTIMATES OF BIVARIATE AUTOREGRESSION
UNRESTRICTED AND RESTRICTED

j	1	2	3	4	Row Sum
		Unrestricted Estimates			
α_j	-0.06783	-0.15063	-0.06351	-0.00627	-0.28824
β_j	0.30407	0.22275	0.15479	-0.02938	0.65223
γ_j	0.70532	0.43141	0.27823	0.00165	1.41661
δ_j	-0.44493	-0.31663	-0.16010	0.03287	-0.88879

$$\hat{V} = \begin{pmatrix} 1.573*10^{-4} & 9.831*10^{-5} \\ & 1.154*10^{-4} \end{pmatrix} \qquad |\hat{V}| = 8.488*10^{-9}$$

Maximum Likelihood Estimates
b=1

j	1	2	3	4	Row Sum
α_j	-0.56630	-0.62942	-0.49703	-0.39033	-2.08308
β_j	0.70566	0.66585	0.54469	0.14558	2.06178
γ_j	0.23349	0.04501	-0.00001	0.00329	0.28178
δ_j	-0.12809	-0.01655	-0.00303	-0.00123	-0.14890

$$\hat{V} = \begin{pmatrix} 1.732*10^{-4} & 1.179*10^{-4} \\ & 1.362*10^{-4} \end{pmatrix} \qquad |\hat{V}| = 9.680*10^{-9}$$

Likelihood ratio statistic = 26.545
Marginal significance level = 0.00085

Maximum Likelihood Estimates
b free

j	1	2	3	4	Row Sum
α_j	-0.48035	-0.63593	-0.54612	-0.38979	-2.05219
β_j	0.69258	0.65924	0.52844	0.15190	2.03216
γ_j	0.31682	0.07705	-0.00284	-0.01249	.37854
δ_j	-0.18501	-0.02871	0.01123	0.00487	- .19762

b = 0.66335

$$\hat{V} = \begin{pmatrix} 1.700*10^{-4} & 1.130*10^{-5} \\ & 1.296*10^{-4} \end{pmatrix} \qquad |\hat{V}| = 9.280*10^{-9}$$

Likelihood ratio statistic = 18.019
Marginal significance level = 0.02108

TABLE 16

CANADA: ESTIMATES OF BIVARIATE AUTOREGRESSION
UNRESTRICTRED AND RESTRICTED

j	1	2	3	4	Row Sum
	Unrestricted Estimates				
α_j	0.14948	0.07733	0.05981	-0.18817	0.09845
β_j	0.07164	-0.07935	0.02268	0.09671	0.11168
γ_j	0.82945	0.30516	0.15284	-0.02884	1.25861
δ_j	-0.45814	-0.26949	-0.11163	0.04070	-0.79856

$$\hat{V} = \begin{pmatrix} 2.199*10^{-5} & 1.114*10^{-5} \\ & 1.240*10^{-5} \end{pmatrix} \qquad |\hat{V}| = 1.499*10^{-10}$$

Maximum Likelihood Estimates
b=1

j	1	2	3	4	Row Sum
α_j	-0.46541	-0.06324	0.25763	-0.11134	-0.38236
β_j	0.39378	-0.11220	-0.06007	-0.02458	0.19693
γ_j	0.26696	-0.01351	-0.07107	0.02913	0.21151
δ_j	-0.11470	0.01886	0.01490	0.00643	-0.07451

$$\hat{V} = \begin{pmatrix} 2.668*10^{-5} & 1.508*10^{-5} \\ & 1.644*10^{-5} \end{pmatrix} \qquad |\hat{V}| = 2.144*10^{-10}$$

Likelihood ratio statistic - 72.246
Marginal significance level = 0.0001

Maximum Likelihood Estimates
b free

j	1	2	3	4	Row Sum
α_j	-0.47036	-0.11258	0.20141	-0.11788	-0.49941
β_j	0.37960	-0.07881	-0.07815	0.01220	0.23484
γ_j	0.29606	-0.00506	-0.06488	0.03605	0.26217
δ_j	-0.15633	0.02658	0.02424	-0.00374	-0.10925

b = 0.87230

$$\hat{V} = \begin{pmatrix} 2.704*10^{-5} & 1.511*10^{-5} \\ & 1.616*10^{-5} \end{pmatrix} \qquad |\hat{V}| = 2.085*10^{-10}$$

Likelihood ratio statistic = 66.696
Marginal significance level = 0.0001

TABLE 17

SWITZERLAND: ESTIMATES OF BIVARIATE AUTOREGRESSION
UNRESTRICTED AND RESTRICTED

j	1	2	3	4	Row Sum
		Unrestricted Estimates			
α_j	-0.09582	0.00814	-0.01271	-0.01044	-0.11083
β_j	0.09477	0.08734	0.10093	-0.07744	0.20560
γ_j	0.82700	0.80629	0.34803	0.00003	1.98135
δ_j	-0.83059	-0.50919	-0.16071	-0.08883	-1.58932

$$\hat{V} = \begin{pmatrix} 2.158*10^{-4} & 1.193*10^{-4} \\ & 1.696*10^{-4} \end{pmatrix} \quad |\hat{V}| = 2.237*10^{-8}$$

Maximum Likelihood Estimates
b=1

j	1	2	3	4	Row Sum
α_j	-0.41943	-0.17910	0.06281	-0.16359	-0.69931
β_j	0.36243	0.09490	0.04269	0.09038	0.08255
γ_j	0.20600	0.03741	-0.03392	0.04641	0.25590
δ_j	-0.14204	-0.01189	-0.00320	-0.02565	-0.18278

$$\hat{V} = \begin{pmatrix} 2.419*10^{-4} & 1.492*10^{-4} \\ & 2.390*10^{-4} \end{pmatrix} \quad |\hat{V}| = 3.555*10^{-8}$$

Likelihood ratio statistic - 93.570
Marginal significance level = 0.0001

Maximum Likelihood Estimates
b free

j	1	2	3	4	Row Sum
α_j	-0.62217	-0.50351	-0.09868	-0.13233	-1.35669
β_j	0.50449	0.36383	0.12815	0.13226	1.12873
γ_j	0.41899	0.23797	-0.00424	0.08930	0.74202
δ_j	-0.40328	-0.12797	-0.01568	-0.08925	-0.63618

b = 0.69214

$$\hat{V} = \begin{pmatrix} 2.649*10^{-4} & 1.498*10^{-4} \\ & 1.993*10^{-4} \end{pmatrix} \quad |\hat{V}| = 3.035*10^{-8}$$

Likelihood ratio statistic = 61.599
Marginal significance level = 0.0001

TABLE 18

UNITED KINGDOM: ESTIMATES OF BIVARIATE AUTOREGRESSION
UNRESTRICTED AND RESTRICTED

j	1	2	3	4	Row Sum
		Unrestricted Estimates			
α_j	-0.02734	0.11613	0.04996	-0.00269	0.13606
β_j	0.07475	0.02602	-0.13810	0.32083	0.28350
γ_j	0.69528	0.47395	0.26807	-0.00221	1.43509
δ_j	-0.50338	-0.34317	-0.22520	0.31747	-0.75428

$$\hat{V} = \begin{pmatrix} 1.055*10^{-4} & 6.942*10^{-5} \\ & 7.122*10^{-5} \end{pmatrix} \qquad |\hat{V}| = 2.695*10^{-9}$$

Maximum Likelihood Estimates
b=1

j	1	2	3	4	Row Sum
α_j	-0.63784	-0.44721	-0.03676	-0.12006	-1.24187
β_j	0.52810	0.28584	0.09796	0.10231	1.01421
γ_j	0.25553	0.14629	-0.02008	0.04839	0.43013
δ_j	-0.22631	-0.06691	-0.00974	-0.04123	-0.34419

$$\hat{V} = \begin{pmatrix} 2.682*10^{-4} & 1.657*10^{-4} \\ & 2.224*10^{-4} \end{pmatrix} \qquad |\hat{V}| = 3.217*10^{-8}$$

Likelihood ratio statistic = 500.886
Marginal significance level = 0.0001

Maximum Likelihood Estimates
b free

j	1	2	3	4	Row Sum
α_j	-0.5770	-0.1623	0.0426	-0.0297	-0.7264
β_j	0.5073	0.0729	-0.0625	-0.0607	0.4570
γ_j	0.0936	0.0080	-0.0041	0.0030	0.1005
δ_j	-0.0263	-0.0237	0.0069	0.0062	-0.0369

b = 0.8697

$$\hat{V} = \begin{pmatrix} 1.301*10^{-4} & 9.136*10^{-5} \\ & 9.283*10^{-5} \end{pmatrix} \qquad |\hat{V}| = 3.733*10^{-9}$$

Likelihood ratio statistic - 65.814
Marginal significance level

f will be higher next period. For the unrestricted estimates, the sum of the α's and β's (the parameters of the s_t equation) and the sum of the γ's and δ's (the parameters of the f_t equation) are both positive. This fact, in conjunction with the previous facts, indicate that the positive "cross" effects dominate the negative "own" effects. However, when we examine the restricted (b=1) estimates, we observe a difference. In this case, the sum of the parameters of the s_t equation is negative, while the sum of the parameters of the f_t equation is positive. That is, for the restricted estimates, the negative "own" effects dominate the positive "cross" effects for the s_t equation, but not for the f_t equation. Finally, both the sum of the parameters of the f_t equation decrease in going from the unrestricted to the restricted estimates.

One final statistic can be reported. Assume we impose the hypothesis that the market is efficient, but b$\neq$1, we can then ask: how much are we hurt by then requiring b=1? This can be answered by comparing $|\hat{V}|$ for b free with $|\hat{V}|$ for b=1. The likelihood ratio statistic, $T[\ln(|V|, b=1) - \ln (|V|, b \text{ free})]$, is distributed $\chi^2(1)$. The test statistic and marginal significance level, in parenthesis, is the Netherlands: 3.273 (0.070); Germany: 8.524 (0.004); Canada: 5.637 (0.0176); Switzerland: 31.945 (0.000).

2.5 Conclusions

Many studies of the foreign exchange market assume that the market is efficient. This implies that there are no unexploited profit opportunities. In terms of the foreign exchange market, this means that the forward rate summarizes all relevant, and available, information about the future spot rate. If one desires to test such an assumption, one requires an equilibrium model of pricing in the foreign exchange market which includes specifying an

information set. Consequently, any empirical test of market efficiency is
a joint test of market efficiency and the equilibrium model being used.
Therefore, a rejection of the empirical test may reflect a rejection of
market efficiency, or rejection of the model being used, or both.

In the first section of this chapter, where we examined the regression $\ln S_{t+4} = a + b \ln F_t + u_{t+4}$, we had mixed, but generally favorable
results. For Canada, Switzerland and the U.K., we found that we could not
reject $a = 0$, $b = 1$; for the Netherlands and Germany, we were able to reject
$a = 0$, $b = 1$. More importantly, for the Netherlands, Germany and Switzerland,
the residuals behaved in a random fashion, indicating that the forward rate
does summarize all available information. Canada and the U.K., on the other
hand, had a significant $Q(12)$ statistic, indicating a departure from randomness. When we restrict $b=1$, the constant term is insignificantly different
from zero and the residuals behave in a similar fashion to when b was free.
We also found that the current forward rate is a more efficient forecast
of the future spot rate than is the current spot rate.

In the second section of this chapter where we examined a bivariate
autoregression for $(\ln S_t - \ln S_{t-1}, \ln F_t - \ln F_{t-1})$, the results were un-
favorable. A point to note is that the null hypotheses is a single point in
the entire parameter space. A relevant question becomes: what model do we
accept as an alternative. As Zvi Griliches says: it takes a model to reject a model. All we have shown is that the model proposed is not compatible
with the data. What are some of the possible reasons for this?

The reason could be purely econometric: For example, was (s_t, f_t) a
linearly indeterministic stationary stochastic process? The simple evidence
indicates that s_t and f_t were stationary. However, we saw in Section 2.3
that σ_ε^2 was not constant over the sample period and so (s_t, f_t) might not
have been stationary: the variance may not have been constant over time.

The other reason relies on questioning the theory that was used in developing the hypotheses to be tested. As Michael Jensen stated, in a slightly different context (1978, p. 95): ". . . as our econometric sophistication increases, we are beginning to find inconsistencies that our cruder data and techniques missed in the past," and "the eventual resolution of these anomalies will result in more precise and more general theories of market efficiency and equilibrium models of the determination of asset prices under uncertainty" (Jensen 1978, p. 96).

The theory being tested relies on the assumption of a constant risk premium. If the risk premium was not constant—perhaps it followed some (low order) stochastic process or was a function of other variables—then the model was misspecified. In addition, Harris and Purvis (1978) construct a model in which a distinction is drawn between permanent and transitory shocks. Consider, for example, a permanent shock such as the oil crisis. People initially interpreted this as a temporary shock, and only over time was it perceived to be a permanent shock. It is only over time, while people accumulated new information, that the exchange rate (gradually) attained its new level. Consequently, looking at a time series we observe serial correlation. However, this serial correlation simply reflects people eliminating their initial confusion of whether the oil shock was permanent or transitory; it does not represent irrational behavior.

Finally, much of the theory is taken from the theory of efficient markets in finance (see Fama 1969). However, there are a number of differences between domestic and international markets. The foreign exchange market is much less regulated than the U.S. stock market. In addition, there are two governments involved in a foreign exchange transaction. There is also much more government intervention in terms of manipulating exchange rates (asset prices) than in the U.S. stock market.

CHAPTER III

THE TERM STRUCTURE OF THE FORWARD PREMIUM

3.1 Introduction

As noted in Chapter I, there exists a multiplicity of maturities of the forward exchange rate. The previous chapter examined the implications of market efficiency for one of these maturities--the one month forward rate. The hypothesis of efficiency also has analogous implications for the relationship between the other maturities and the spot rate. In addition, efficiency has implications for the joint behavior of these other maturities. This chapter will theoretically and empirically examine these additional implications.

Section 3.2 will propose an equilibrium theory of the term structure of the forward premium. By combining the (certainty equivalence) theory of the term structure of (domestic and foreign) interest rates with the hypothesis of interest rate parity, a simple expression relating the six month forward premium to the expected future one month forward premium can be derived. It will be shown that the six month forward premium can be written as a geometric average of expected future one month forward premiums. In Section 3.3 it is shown that a convenient and efficient method to extract the expected one month forward premium can be obtained by assuming that a general (bivariate) stochastic process generates the one and six month forward premiums. The theory developed in Section 3.2 will then impose highly nonlinear cross equation restrictions on the parameters of the stochastic process.

55

The restrictions imposed on the parameters of the model by the economic theory are highly nonlinear. Sections 3.4 and 3.5 discuss two methods of testing the validity of the restrictions. Section 3.4 provides a statistical test of the hypothesis that requires only the unrestricted estimates. The rejection region, under the null hypothesis, is derived. The statistical test proposed in Section 3.5 requires the restricted parameter estimates. Maximum likelihood methods for estimating the constrained models are discussed and implemented.

In the previous chapter, the German-U.S. foreign exchange market was found to be (marginally) efficient--the slope was significantly less than one and the constant was significantly different from zero, although the residuals indicated that the forward rate summarized all available information about the future spot rate. The Canadian-U.S. foreign exchange market appears to be inefficient--the forward rate provides an unbiased estimate of the future spot rate, but it did not summarize all available information. In this sense, Germany and Canada span the set of foreign exchange markets. Because of this, and the high cost of computing, we shall focus on the German-U.S. and the Canadian-U.S. foreign exchange markets.

3.2 The Economics of the Term Structure of the Forward Premium

To develop a theory of the term structure of the forward premium, we begin by assuming that interest rate parity holds. There is much empirical evidence in support of this condition (Frenkel and Levich 1975, 1977). Interest rate parity states that the expected rate of depreciation on foreign exchange equals the interest rate differential. We can write this as:

$$\frac{1 + I_{n,t}}{1 + I^*_{n,t}} = \frac{E_t S_{t+n}}{S_t} \tag{3.1}$$

$$1 + i_{n,t} = \frac{(1 + I_{n,t})^n}{(1 + I_{n-1,t})^{n-1}} \qquad (3.2a)$$

$$(1 + I_{n,t})^n = (1 + i_{1,t})(1 + i_{2,t}) \cdots (1 + i_{n,t}) \qquad (3.2b)$$

where $I_{n,t}$ = n period rate of interest at period t

$i_{n,t}$ = implicit one period forward interest rate for period $t+n$.

Dividing by the foreign country version of (3.2a), (3.2a*), yields:

$$\frac{1 + i_n}{1 + i_n^*} = \left[\frac{1 + I_n}{1 + I_n^*}\right]^n \bigg/ \left[\frac{1 + I_{n-1}}{1 + I_{n-1}^*}\right]^{n-1} \qquad (3.3)$$

Substituting interest rate parity (3.1) into (3.3) and cancelling yields:

$$\frac{E_t S_{t+n}}{E_t S_{t+n-1}} = \frac{1 + i_n}{1 + i_n^*} = 1 + E_t \bar{r}_{1,t+n-1} \qquad (3.4)$$

$E_t \bar{r}_{1,t+n-1}$ is the implied expected change in the spot exchange rate in period $t+n$. Dividing (3.2b) by (3.2b*), equating to (3.3) and substituting from (3.4) yields:

$$\frac{E_t S_{t+n}}{S_t} = \frac{(1 + i_1)(1 + i_2) \cdots (1 + i_n)}{(1 + i_1^*)(1 + i_2^*) \cdots (1 + i_n^*)}$$

$$= (1 + \bar{r}_{1,t})(1 + E_t \bar{r}_{I,t+1}) \cdots (1 + E_t \bar{r}_{1,t+n-1}). \qquad (3.5)$$

Define

$$r_{1,t} = \left[\frac{F_{1,t}}{S_t}\right] - 1$$

where $F_{1,t}$ is the one month forward prevailing at time t, and $r_{1,t}$ is the one month forward premium, at time t. If we assume that the forward rate is an unbiased predictor of the future spot rate, we have

$$E_t S_{t+1} = F_{1,t}. \tag{3.7}$$

Substituting equation (3.7) into (3.6), we obtain

$$r_{1,t} = \left[\frac{E_t S_{t+1}}{S_t}\right] - 1.$$

But, $\bar{r}_{1,t}$ is also the implied expected change in the spot rate, hence we have that

$$r_{1,t} = E_t \bar{r}_{1,t} = \left[\frac{E_t S_{t+1}}{S_t}\right] - 1 \tag{3.8}$$

Finally, define the n period forward premium as

$$r_{n,t} = \left[\frac{F_{n,t}}{S_t}\right]^{1/n} - 1.$$

Assuming that (3.7) holds for maturities other than one period, that is, $E_t S_{t+n} = F_{n,t}$, we obtain that

$$r_{n,t} = E_t \bar{r}_{n,t} = \left[\frac{E_t S_{t+n}}{S_t}\right]^{1/n} - 1. \tag{3.9}$$

Substituting the definition of $r_{1,t}$ (3.8) and $r_{n,t}$ (3.9) into (3.5), yields

$$(1 + r_{n,t})^n = (1 + r_{1,t})(1 + E_r{}_{1,t+1}) \cdots (1 + E_t r_{1,t+n-1})$$

or, as an approximation (using $\ln(1+x) \doteq x$, for small x)

$$r_{n,t} = \frac{1}{n} [r_{1,t} + E_t r_{1,t+1} + \cdots + E_t r_{1,t+n-1}] \tag{3.10}$$

E_t is the mathematical expectations operator conditional on the set of information available to economic agents at time t, Ω_t. We will assume that

$\Omega_t \supseteq \Omega_{t-1} \supseteq \cdots$, and that Ω_t contains at least all current and lagged values of $(r_{1,t}, r_{n,t})$.

To add empirical content to equation (3.10), we must specify how expectations are formed and what variables belong in Ω_t. First, notice that the conditional expectations operator in (3.10), E_t, has Ω_t as the conditioning set, where Ω_t includes all relevant information for calculating expectations of future one month rates of depreciation. For convenience in deriving testable implications based on (3.10), let us write $E_t x_s$ as $E(x_s | \Omega_t)$, and so rewrite (3.10) as

$$r_{n,t} = \frac{1}{n} [r_{1,t} + E(r_{1,t+1} | \Omega_t) + \cdots + E(r_{1,t+n-1} | \Omega_t)] \qquad (3.10')$$

Let θ_t be any subset of Ω_t, such that θ_t includes at least current and lagged values of $r_{1,t}$ and $r_{n,t}$. Now, take expectations of both sides of (3.10'), conditional on the __smaller__ information set θ_t, to obtain

$$r_{n,t} = \frac{1}{n} [r_{1,t} + E(r_{1,t+1} | \theta_t) + \cdots + E(r_{1,t+n-1} | \theta_t)] \qquad (3.10'')$$

where we used the law of iterated projections that states that $E(y|z) = E\{E(y|x,z)|z\}$, where x, y, z are normal random variables. Notice that (3.10'') and (3.10') are of the same form. In particular, if we leave important variables out of θ_t (that were in Ω_t) we will not invalidate the tests reported. Now, take first differences of (3.10''):

$$r_{n,t} - r_{n,t-1} = \frac{1}{n} \{ (r_{1,t} - r_{1,t-1}) + [E(r_{1,t+1} | \theta_t)$$
$$- E(r_{1,t} | \theta_{t-1})] + \cdots + [E(r_{1,t+n-1} | \theta_t) \qquad (3.11)$$
$$- E(r_{1,t+n-2} | \theta_{t-1})] \}.$$

Write $\Delta r_{n,t} = r_{n,t} - r_{n,t-1}$ and $\Delta r_{1,t} = r_{1,t} - r_{1,t-1}$. Take expectations of both sides of (3.11), conditional on θ_{t-1}, using the law of iterated pro-jections, to get

$$E(\Delta r_{n,t})|\theta_{t-1}) = \frac{1}{n} \{E(\Delta r_{1,t}|\theta_{t-1}) + E(\Delta r_{1,t+1}|\theta_{t-1}) + \ldots +$$

$$\text{(3.11')}$$

$$E(\Delta r_{1,t+n-1}|\theta_{t-1})\}.$$

We must now specify <u>exactly</u> which variables to include in θ_t. We shall restrict θ_t to include only current and lagged values of $\Delta r_{1,t}$, $\Delta r_{n,t}$, that is, $\theta_t = \{\Delta r_{1,t},\ \Delta r_{1,t-1},\ \ldots\ ,\ \Delta r_{n,t},\ \Delta r_{n,t-1},\ \ldots\}$. Given this information set, we can easily calculate the conditional expectations in (3.11'). We shall report two methods of calculating these expectations, and the restrictions implied by (3.11').

3.3 The Empirical Implications of the Term Structure of the Forward Premium

Assuming that $(\Delta r_{1,t},\ \Delta r_{n,t})$ is a linearly indeterministic co-variance stationary stochastic process, we can use the Wold Decomposition Theorem to write (letting $R_{1,t} = \Delta r_{1,t}$ and $R_{n,t} = \Delta r_{n,t}$):

$$R_{1,t} = \alpha(L)w_t + \beta(L)v_t$$

$$\text{(3.12)}$$

$$R_{n,t} = \gamma(L)w_t + \delta(L)v_t$$

where $\alpha(L)$, $\beta(L)$, $\gamma(L)$ and $S(L)$ are one sided polynomials in the lag operator

$$w_t = R_{1,t} - E(R_{1,t}|\theta_{t-1})$$

$$v_t = R_{n,t} - E(R_{n,t}|\theta_{t-2})$$

$$Ew_t w_{t-k} = \begin{cases} \sigma_w^2 & k = 0 \\ 0 & k \neq 0 \end{cases}$$

$$Ev_t v_{t-k} = \begin{cases} \sigma_v^2 & k = 0 \\ 0 & k \neq 0 \end{cases}$$

$$Ew_t v_{t-k} = \begin{cases} \sigma_{wv} & k = 0 \\ 0 & k \neq 0 \end{cases}$$

$$\alpha(0) = \delta(0) = 1 \text{ and } \beta(0) = \gamma(0) = 0.$$

The Weiner-Kolmogorov prediction formulas allow us to write the conditional expectations in (3.11') in a simple fashion:

$$E_{t-1}R_{1,t+k} = \left[\frac{\alpha(L)}{L^{k+1}}\right]_+ w_{t-1} + \left[\frac{\beta(L)}{L^{k+1}}\right]_+ v_{t-1} \qquad (3.13)$$

where $[\ ]_+$ means "ignore negative powers of L." Substituting expression (3.13) into (3.11') and rearranging, yields:

$$\begin{aligned}
E_{t-1}R_{n,t} &= \frac{1}{n}\left[\frac{\alpha(L)}{L} + \frac{\alpha(L)}{L^2} + \cdots + \frac{\alpha(L)}{L^n}\right]_+ w_{t-1} \\
&\quad + \frac{1}{n}\left[\frac{\beta(L)}{L} + \frac{\beta(L)}{L^2} + \cdots + \frac{\beta(L)}{L^n}\right]_+ v_{t-1} \qquad (3.14) \\
&= \frac{1}{n}\left[\frac{\alpha(L)}{L}\left(\frac{1-L^n}{1-L^{-1}}\right)\right]_+ w_{t-1} + \frac{1}{n}\left[\frac{\beta(L)}{L}\left(\frac{1-L^{-n}}{1-L^{-1}}\right)\right]_+ v_{t-1}.
\end{aligned}$$

But, we can also use the Weinter-Kolmogorov prediction formula to write the left hand side of (3.14) as

$$E_{t-1}R_{n,t} = \left[\frac{\gamma(L)}{L}\right]_+ w_{t-1} + \left[\frac{\delta(L)}{L}\right]_+ v_{t-1}. \qquad (3.15)$$

Equating terms in (3.14) and (3.15) yield a set of cross equation restrictions on the parameters of the bivariate moving average representation of $(R_{1,t}, R_{n,t})$ in (3.12) implied by the theory of the term structure of the forward premium:

$$\left[\frac{\gamma(L)}{L}\right]_+ = \frac{1}{n}\left[\frac{\alpha(L)}{L}\left(\frac{1-L^{-n}}{1-L^{-1}}\right)\right]_+$$

$$\left[\frac{\delta(L)}{L}\right]_+ = \frac{1}{n}\left[\frac{\beta(L)}{L}\left(\frac{1-L^{-n}}{1-L^{-1}}\right)\right]_+ . \tag{3.16}$$

As in the last chapter, it would be possible to estimate (3.12) subject to (3.16) and so test the validity of the restrictions embodied in (3.16). However, as before, it is very difficult to estimate bivariate moving averages and so we use an alternative representation of $(R_{1,t}, R_{n,t})$.

Equation (3.11') is a restriction across the systematic part of $(R_{1,t}, R_{n,t})$, imposed by rational expectations. By our assumptions of stationarity we can write $(R_{1,t}, R_{n,t})$ as a vector autoregression (where the α's, β's, γ's and δ's in (3.17) are different than those in (3.12), the w_t and v_t are the same):

$$R_{1,t} = \sum_{i=1}^{M} \alpha_i R_{1,t-i} + \sum_{i=1}^{M} \beta_i R_{n,t-i} + w_t \tag{3.17a}$$

$$R_{n,t} = \sum_{i=1}^{M} \gamma_i R_{1,t-i} + \sum_{i=1}^{M} \delta_i R_{n,t-i} + v_t \tag{3.17b}$$

where

$$Ew_t R_{1,t-i} = Ev_t R_{1,t-i} = Ew_t R_{n,t-i} =$$

$$Ev_t R_{n,t-i} = 0, \quad \text{for } i = 1, 2, \dots, M$$

$$Ew_t v_{t-i} = \begin{cases} 0 & i \neq 0 \\ \sigma_{wv} & i = 0 \end{cases}$$

$\{w_t, v_t\}$ is the innovation in the $(R_{1,t}, R_{n,t})$ process; the errors are contemporaneously correlated, but uncorrelated at all lags. Equation (3.17) can be rewritten as:[1]

---

[1] Equation (3.18) amounts to rewriting an Mth order difference equation as a vector first order system.

$$x_t = Ax_{t-1} + a_t \qquad (3.18)$$

where

$$x_t = \begin{vmatrix} R_{1,t} \\ R_{1,t-1} \\ \cdot \\ \cdot \\ \cdot \\ R_{1,t-M+1} \\ R_{n,t} \\ R_{n,t-1} \\ \cdot \\ \cdot \\ \cdot \\ R_{n,t-M+1} \end{vmatrix} \qquad a_t = \begin{vmatrix} w_t \\ 0 \\ \cdot \\ \cdot \\ \cdot \\ 0 \\ v_t \\ 0 \\ \cdot \\ \cdot \\ \cdot \\ 0 \end{vmatrix}$$

$$A = \begin{vmatrix} \alpha_1 & \alpha_2 & \cdots & \alpha_{M-1} & \alpha_M & \beta_1 & \beta_2 & \cdots & \beta_{M-1} & \beta_M \\ 1 & 0 & \ldots & 0 & 0 & 0 & 0 & \ldots & 0 & 0 \\ \cdot & \cdot & & \cdot & \cdot & \cdot & \cdot & & \cdot & \cdot \\ \cdot & \cdot & & \cdot & \cdot & \cdot & \cdot & & \cdot & \cdot \\ \cdot & \cdot & & \cdot & \cdot & \cdot & \cdot & & \cdot & \cdot \\ 0 & 0 & \ldots & 1 & 0 & 0 & 0 & \ldots & 0 & 0 \\ \gamma_1 & \gamma_2 & \cdots & \gamma_{M-1} & \gamma_M & \delta_1 & \delta_2 & \cdots & \delta_{M-1} & \delta_M \\ 0 & 0 & \ldots & 0 & 0 & 1 & 0 & \ldots & 0 & 0 \\ \cdot & \cdot & & \cdot & \cdot & \cdot & \cdot & & \cdot & \cdot \\ \cdot & \cdot & & \cdot & \cdot & \cdot & \cdot & & \cdot & \cdot \\ 0 & 0 & \ldots & 0 & 0 & 0 & 0 & \ldots & 1 & 0 \end{vmatrix} \begin{matrix} \\ \\ \\ \\ \\ \\ \leftarrow \text{row } M+1 \\ \\ \\ \\ \leftarrow \text{row } 2M. \end{matrix}$$

Repeated substitution from (3.18) yields:

$$x_{t+1} = Ax_t + a_{t+1} = A^2 x_{t-1} + Aa_t + a_{t+1}$$

$$x_{t+j} = A^{j+1} x_{t-1} + A^j a_t + \ldots + a_{t+j}. \qquad (3.19)$$

64

Since $E_{t-1}a_{t+k} = 0$ ($k = 0, 1, \ldots$) we can write (3.19) as

$$E_{t-1}x_{t+j} = A^{j+1}x_{t-1} \qquad j = 1, 2, \ldots \tag{3.20}$$

Letting $c = (1 \ 0 \ \ldots \ 0)$ and $d = (0 \ \ldots \ 0 \ 1 \ 0 \ \ldots \ 0)$, we can write

$$\uparrow \text{ column } M + 1$$

$$R_{1,t} = c \ x_t$$

$$R_{n,t} = d \ x_t. \tag{3.21}$$

Multiply (3.18) by c and d, to get

$$c \ x_t = c \ Ax_{t-1} + c \ a_t$$

$$d \ x_t = d \ Ax_{t-1} + d \ a_t.$$

Equating to (3.21) we get

$$R_{1,t} = c \ Ax_{t-1} + a_{1,t}$$

$$R_{n,t} = d \ Ax_{t-1} + a_{n,t}. \tag{3.22}$$

Multiply restriction (3.20) by c to get

$$E_{t-1}c \ x_{t+j} = c \ A^{j+1}x_{t-1} \qquad j = 1, 2, \ldots \tag{3.23}$$

Updating (3.21) by $+j$ and substituting into (3.23) yields

$$E_{t-1}R_{1,t+j} = c \ A^{j+1}x_{t-1} \qquad j = 1, 2, \ldots \tag{3.24}$$

Substitution of (3.24) into (3.11) yields

$$E_{t-1}R_{n,t} = (1/n)(cAx_{t-1} + cA^2x_{t-1} + \ldots + cA^nx_{t-1})$$

$$= (1/n) \ c(A + A^2 + \ldots + A^n)x_{t-1}. \tag{3.25}$$

Taking expectations conditional on I_{t-1} in (3.22) yields

$$E_{t-1}R_{n,t} = d\, Ax_{t-1}. \tag{3.26}$$

Equating equations (3.25) and (3.26) yields the following restriction imposed by rational expectations:

$$d\, A = (1/n)\, c(A + A^2 + \ldots + A^n). \tag{3.27}$$

The intuition behind these restrictions arise from the following observations. We assumed that the $(R_{1,t}, R_{n,t})$ process was generated by a vector autoregression. That is, we regress both $R_{1,t}$ and $R_{n,t}$ against lagged values of $(R_{1,t}, R_{n,t})$. Wold has shown the conditions under which this is valid (see Whittle 1963). If the economic agents realize this they will use the parameters of the autoregression to generate their forecasts. For the data to be consistent with the model the parameter values must be restricted. These restrictions are summarized in equation (3.11) and equivalently in equation (3.27).

3.4 Econometric Tests and Results, I

The restrictions implied by equation (3.27) are highly nonlinear. There are two basic methods to test the validity of the restrictions implied by the theory. The first method, discussed in detail in this section, was originally proposed by Wald. This method requires obtaining the unrestricted maximum likelihood estimates $\hat{\psi}^u$ of the parameter vector $\psi = (\alpha, \beta, \gamma, \delta)$. Let us write the restrictions implied by (3.27) in the form $h(\psi) = 0$. Wald's method then tests $h(\hat{\psi}^u) = 0$. The second method, discussed in detail in the next section is based on the likelihood ratio test. This method requires obtaining in addition to the unrestricted estimate, $\hat{\psi}^u$, the restricted estimate $\hat{\psi}^r$. One then compares the likelihood

of $\hat{\psi}^u$ to $\hat{\psi}^r$. A difficulty with this method is obtaining the restricted
maximum likelihood estimates. The next section will present two methods
of obtaining $\hat{\psi}^r$.

Under the assumption that $\{w_t, v_t\}$ is bivariate normal, the likelihood function for a sample of $\{w_t, v_t\}$, $t = 1, 2, \ldots T$ is given by

$$L(\alpha, \beta, \gamma, \delta) = (2\pi)^{-T}|V|^{-T/2} \exp\{-\frac{1}{2} \sum_{t=1}^{T} e_t' V^{-1} e_t\} \qquad (3.28)$$

where
$$e_t = \begin{bmatrix} w_t \\ v_t \end{bmatrix} \qquad V = E \; e_t' \; e_t.$$

Maxmimizing (3.28) without any restrictions, that is, with all parameters
free, is equivalent to estimating (3.17) by least squares. Wilson (1973)
shows that the parameter estimates with an unknown V may be obtained by

$$\min |\hat{V}| = | \; (1/T) \sum_{t=1}^{T} \hat{e}_t \; \hat{e}_t' \; |.$$

To test restriction (3.17) we proceed as follows. Lèt

$$\psi = (\underline{\alpha}', \; \underline{\beta}', \; \underline{\gamma}'. \; \underline{\delta}')$$

$$\hat{\psi}^u = \text{OLS (unrestricted) estimate.}$$

Write restriction (3.27) as

$$h(\psi) = dA(\psi) - (1/n)c(A(\psi) + A^2(\psi) + \ldots + A^n(\psi)) \qquad (3.29)$$

$$= (0 \; 0 \; \ldots \; 0) = \underline{0}$$

where we write $A = A(\psi)$ to indicate the dependence of A on ψ. The test
amounts to testing whether the vector $h(\hat{\psi})$ is significantly different from
the zero vector. The problem is to determine the shape of the rejection

region. The problem is solved as follows (Silvey 1975, pp. 115-116, or Rao 1973, pp. 418-419):

We expect $\underline{\psi}^u$ to be "close to" $\underline{\psi}$, under the null hypothesis, and, we know that $\sqrt{n}(\underline{\psi}^u - \underline{\psi})$ is approximately $N(0, B_\psi^{-1})$, where B_ψ^{-1} is the information matrix for the coefficient vector $\underline{\psi}$, in a single observation. Expanding $h(\psi)$ about $\underline{\psi}$ in a Taylor series, to linear terms, we get

$$h(\hat{\underline{\psi}}) \approx h(\underline{\psi}) + H_\psi'(\hat{\underline{\psi}} - \underline{\psi}) \qquad (3.30)$$

where
$$H_\psi = \left[\frac{\partial h_j(\psi)}{\partial \psi_i}\right].$$

Since $h(\underline{\psi}) = 0$, under the null hypothesis, we may rewrite (3.30) as

$$h(\hat{\underline{\psi}}) \approx H_\psi' \, (\hat{\underline{\psi}} - \underline{\psi}). \qquad (3.31)$$

Therefore, $\sqrt{n} \, h(\hat{\psi})$ is approximately $N(0, H_\psi' \, B_\psi^{-1} \, H_\psi)$. Letting x be the vector of observations, the rejection region becomes

$$\{x \,|\, n[h(\psi(x))'(H_\psi' \, B_\psi^{-1} \, H_\psi)^{-1} \, h(\psi(x))] > k\}. \qquad (3.32)$$

To actually apply this test one needs an estimate of H_ψ and B_ψ^{-1}. For $(1/n)B_\psi^{-1}$ we can use the estimated variance-covariance matrix, obtained from estimating (3.17). For H_ψ, we numerically differentiate the 1x8 restriction vector $h(\underline{\psi})$ (at the OLS estimates) with respect to all sixteen parameters. Calling these estimates $(1/n)B_{\hat{\psi}}^{-1}$ and $H_{\hat{\psi}}$, the value W is given by

$$W = h(\psi)'[H_{\hat{\psi}}(1/n)B_{\hat{\psi}}^{-1} \, H_{\hat{\psi}}]h(\psi). \qquad (3.33)$$

Under the null hypothesis, $h(\underline{\psi}) = 0$, W is approximately distributed chi-square with eight degrees of freedom. Large values of W indicate rejection of the hypothesis.

The OLS (unrestricted) estimates are given in Tables 19 and 20, under the heading "Unrestricted Estimates." Also presented is an estimate of V and $|V|$. At the bottom of Tables 19 and 20 the W-statistic is presented, along with its marginal significance level. The marginal significance level is the probability of observing a number greater than the statistic, given that the null hypothesis is true.

The results presented in Table 19 for Germany indicate a failure to reject the validity of the hypothesis that the pure expectations theory of the term structure of the forward premium is correct. The W-statistic of 10.42 is insignificant, as indicated by a marginal significance level of 23.7 percent. The results in Table 20 for Canada indicate rejection of the null hypothesis. The W-statistic of 21.84 is significant, as indicated by a marginal significance level of 0.5 percent. The roots of the characteristic equation indicate that the process is stationary.

3.5 Econometric Tests and Results, II

In the last section, we presented tests of the validity of restriction (3.27), based on the unrestricted estimates. In the case of Canada, we cannot determine the source of rejection. In this section, we shall estimate the model with the restrictions imposed, and then compare the restricted and unrestricted models using a likelihood ratio test.

The restrictions implied by (3.27) are highly nonlinear. Sargent (1979b) proposes two alternative estimation strategies. The first method requires estimating the first row of A, equation (3.17a), by least squares. Then, the (M+1)st row of A, equation (3 17b), is calculated using an iterative procedure. Form a preliminary estimate of A, call it A_o, by setting row M + 1 to a row of zeroes, and all other rows to their known (or

TABLE 19

GERMANY: ESTIMATES OF BIVARIATE AUTOREGRESSION
UNRESTRICTED AND RESTRICTED

j	1	2	3	4
	Unrestricted Estimates			
α_j	-0.3603	0.0726	-0.0856	-0.2098
β_j	0.5599	-0.5044	0.1862	0.4478
γ_j	-0.0767	0.0642	0.0293	-0.0412
δ_j	0.2227	-0.1829	0.0304	0.1210

$$V = \begin{pmatrix} 7.726*10^{-7} & 2.540*10^{-7} \\ & 1.281*10^{-7} \end{pmatrix} \qquad |V| = 3.442*10^{-14}$$

Restricted Estimates

j	1	2	3	4
α_j	-0.3651	-0.1119	-0.1779	-0.1117
β_j	0.3003	-0.0845	0.2441	0.2275
γ_j	-0.0797	-0.0410	-0.0264	-0.0098
δ_j	0.0784	0.0447	0.0435	0.0199

$$V = \begin{pmatrix} 7.959*10^{-7} & 2.666*10^{-7} \\ & 1.352*10^{-7} \end{pmatrix} \qquad |V| = 3.652*10^{-14}$$

Likelihood ratio statistic = 11.134

Marginal significance level = 0.194

$$W = 10.42$$

Marginal significance level = 0.237

TABLE 20

CANADA: ESTIMATES OF BIVARIATE AUTOREGRESSION
UNRESTRICTED AND RESTRICTED

j	1	2	3	4
		Unrestricted Estimates		
α_j	-0.2830	-0.0174	-0.0168	-0.1421
β_j	0.3743	0.1092	0.1202	0.0028
γ_j	0.1745	0.1186	0.0643	0.0171
δ_j	-0.1140	-0.0249	-0.0161	0.0001

$$\hat{V} = \begin{pmatrix} 9.423*10^{-8} & 4.572*10^{-8} \\ & 4.084*10^{-8} \end{pmatrix} \qquad |\hat{V}| = 1.757*10^{-15}$$

		Restricted Estimates		
α_j	-0.5183	-0.0885	-0.0077	-0.1151
β_j	0.5196	0.0389	0.0769	-0.0012
γ_j	-0.0673	-0.0227	-0.0135	-0.0098
δ_j	0.0580	0.0118	0.0064	-0.0001

$$\hat{V} = \begin{pmatrix} 9.829*10^{-8} & 4.958*10^{-8} \\ & 4.498*10^{-8} \end{pmatrix} \qquad |\hat{V}| = 1.963*10^{-15}$$

Likelihood ratio statistic = 20.843

Marginal significance level = 0.008

$$W = 21.84$$

Marginal significance level = 0.005

consistent) values. Calculate the (M+1)st row of A, at iteration i + 1, as

$$(\text{row M+1})_{i+1} = dA_{i+1} = c \frac{1}{n} [A_i + A_i^2 + \ldots + A_i^{M-1}] \qquad (3.34)$$

where A_i is the estimate of A on the ith iteration. At each step in form-
ing A_{i+1}, all rows (except the (M+1)st) are kept equal to the corresponding
row of A_o. If this procedure converges, it will find an A that satisfies
(3.27). Since the elements of row 1 are consistently estimated by least
squares, the (M+1)st row will be consistently estimated as a function of
the first row of A.

Define the solution to the iteration on (3.34) as the (set) function

$$(\gamma, \delta) = \phi(\alpha, \beta) \qquad (3.35)$$

ϕ maps the α's and β's into a set of γ's and δ's that satisfy restriction
(3.27). Hence, one (consistent) estimator of γ, δ is $\phi(\alpha, \beta)$.

Under the restriction (3.27) the likelihood function in (3.28),
$L(\alpha, \beta, \gamma, \delta | \{s_t\}, \{f_t\})$, becomes a function only of the α's and β's. As
Wilson (1973) argues, maximum likelihood estimates with an unknown V are
obtained by minimizing $|\hat{V}|$, with respect to the α's and β's, where

$$|\hat{V}| = | \frac{1}{T} \sum_{t=1}^{T} e_t(\alpha, \beta) e_t(\alpha, \beta)' |$$

where the $e_t(\alpha, \beta)$, the residuals from (3.17), are functions of the α's and
β's only, since they were calculated from (3.17) with (3.27) imposed.

A derivative free nonlinear minimization routine can be used to
estimate (3.17) under the restriction (3.27). The IMSL subroutine ZXMIN,
which uses a quasi-Newton method, was used. Generally, 600 iterations (at
a cost of $25) was required to obtain three significant digits. The least

squares estimates of α and β were used as starting values.

Tables 19 and 20 report, in addition to the unrestricted ·estimtes, the restricted maximum likelihood estimates. In addition, the likelihood ratio statistic, which is distributed $\chi^2(8)$, is reported along with the marginal significance level.

The results for Germany indicate a failure to reject the null hypothesis. The likelihood ratio statistic of 11.134 is insignificant, as indicated by the marginal significance level of 19.4 percent. The results for Canada, a likelihood ratio statistic of 20.843 (marginal significance level of 0.8 percent), indicate a rejection of the null hypothesis.

Not surprisingly, the results implied by the W-statistic and likelihood ratio statistic are very close (marginal significance levels of 23.7 percent and 19.4 percent for Germany, and 0.5 percent and 0.8 percent for Canada). This is as it should be, since both tests are asymptotically equivalent (Silvey 1970, p. 118), and the sample size is 188 observations.

Can we use the restricted estimates to locate the reason the null hypothesis is rejected for Canada? Table 21 presents an estimate of the variance-covariance matrix of the restricted parameter estimates (α and β) for Canada. Standard errors for γ and δ are not reported since γ and δ cannot be analytically solved for in terms of α and β. The difference between the restricted and unrestricted estimates of α and β are insignificant. Using the standard errors of the unrestricted estimates of γ and δ (not reported), the unrestricted estimate of γ_1 is significantly different from the restricted estimate (all other γ's and δ's are insignificantly different). In calculating the Wald statistic we required an estimate of $h(\psi)$—the restriction vector implied by (3.27). An estimate of that vector, evaluated at the OLS estimate is

TABLE 21

VARIANCE-COVARIANCE MATRIX OF CANADIAN ESTIMATES OF (α, β)

	α_1	α_2	α_3	α_4	β_1	β_2	β_3	β_4
α_1	0.171							
α_2	-0.133	0.605						
α_3	0.007	0.331	0.386					
α_4	0.243	-0.247	0.004	0.523				
β_1	0.035	0.036	-0.005	0.027	0.030			
β_2	-0.228	-0.179	-0.107	-0.221	-0.133	0.683		
β_3	-0.080	0.066	-0.333	-0.116	0.083	-0.072	0.755	
β_4	0.074	-0.115	-0.070	-0.257	0.028	-0.159	-0.115	0.848

$$h = (0.211 \quad 0.129 \quad 0.079 \quad 0.035 \quad -0.185 \quad -0.052 \quad -0.032 \quad -0.00)$$

$$|h - 0| = 0.107.$$

It is interesting to note that the first restriction, $h_1(\psi) = 0.211$, is also the largest in absolute value. Again the results are consistent between the Wald test and likelihood ratio test.

As in the last chapter, we know that there may be a problem with heteroskedasticity. To test this assertion, we split the Canadian sample in two, and reestimated the restricted and unrestricted version of the model. The results are presented in Tables 22 and 23.

For the first period we obtain a likelihood ratio statistic 21.465, with a marginal significance level of 0.6 percent. So, we again reject the

TABLE 22

CANADA: ESTIMATES OF BIVARIATE AUTOREGRESSION
UNRESTRICTED AND RESTRICTED, FIRST PERIOD

j	1	2	3	4
		Unrestricted Estimates		
α_j	−0.5758	−0.2897	−0.3780	−0.4209
β_j	1.0329	0.4575	0.7801	0.0494
γ_j	0.0177	−0.0767	−0.1543	−0.1640
δ_j	0.2066	0.2860	0.3201	0.0760

$$\hat{V} = \begin{pmatrix} 11.125*10^{-8} & 4.6840*10^{-8} \\ & 2.8978*10^{-8} \end{pmatrix} \quad |\hat{V}| = 1.030*10^{-15}$$

		Restricted Estimates		
α_j	−0.7581	−0.2875	−0.1967	−0.2003
β_j	0.9032	0.1384	0.3603	−0.0012
γ_j	−0.0895	−0.0462	−0.0227	−0.0098
δ_j	0.0880	0.0302	0.0176	−0.0001

$$\hat{V} = \begin{pmatrix} 12.691*10^{-8} & 5.748*10^{-8} \\ & 3.631*10^{-9} \end{pmatrix} \quad |\hat{V}| = 1.304*10^{-15}$$

Likelihood ratio statistic = 21.465

Marginal significance level = 0.006

TABLE 23

CANADA: ESTIMATES OF BIVARIATE AUTOREGRESSION
UNRESTRICTED AND RESTRICTED, SECOND PERIOD

j	1	2	3	4
	Unrestricted Estimates			
α_j	−0.0554	0.0691	0.1566	0.2611
β_j	0.0727	−0.0466	−0.1590	−0.1747
γ_j	0.3164	0.2144	0.1989	0.3244
δ_j	−0.2859	−0.1703	−0.1966	−0.1570

$$\hat{V} = \begin{pmatrix} 5.932*10^{-8} & 3.503*10^{-8} \\ & 4.736*10^{-8} \end{pmatrix} \qquad |\hat{V}| = 1.582*10^{-15}$$

	Restricted Estimates			
α_j	−0.1480	0.1212	0.2087	0.2047
β_j	0.1487	−0.0993	−0.1770	−0.1684
γ_j	0.0518	0.0964	0.0822	0.0437
δ_j	−0.0376	−0.0802	−0.0688	−0.0360

$$\hat{V} = \begin{pmatrix} 6.013*10^{-8} & 3.649*10^{-8} \\ & 5.259*10^{-8} \end{pmatrix} \qquad |\hat{V}| = 1.831*10^{-15}$$

Likelihood ratio statistic = 13.302

Marginal significance level = 0.102

null hypothesis for Canada for the first period. The likelihood ratio statistic for the whole period and the first period are quite close. For the second period we obtain a likelihood ratio statistic of only 13.302, with a marginal significance level of 10.2 percent. Therefore, for the second period we fail to reject the null hypothesis, and therefore conclude that the data are consistent with the pure expectations theory of the term structure of the forward premium--for the second period. The roots of the characteristic equation indicate that the process was stationary. As stated in Chapter II, the variance of the forecast error changed over time in the Canadian case. Consequently, the data may not have been stationary and so the econometric methodology may have been suspect. Splitting the sample in two presumably reduced the problem posed by heteroskedasticity.

3.5 Conclusions

Most studies that test foreign exchange market efficiency focus on the relation between the spot exchange rate and a single maturity for the forward exchange rate, usually the one month rate. This procedure ignores the fact that more than one maturity currently is being traded. This chapter extends the analysis of market efficiency so as to obtain implications concerning the joint movements of the spot exchange rate and the one and six month forward exchange rate. Using the certainty equivalence theory of the term structure of (domestic and foreign) interest rates and the hypothesis of interest rate parity, it is possible to write the six month forward premium as a geometric average of the current one month forward premium and expected future one month forward premiums. Testable implications are then derived by assuming that the one and six month forward premiums are generated by a bivariate autoregression.

The hypothesis of rational expectations imposes a set of highly non-linear cross equation restrictions on the parameters of the model. Two different methods were then presented to test the validity of the restrictions. Both methods yielded identical conclusions. It was found that for Germany the data were consistent with the theory of the term structure of the forward premium. For Canada the data were inconsistent with the theory. We had seen in Chapter II that the Canadian-U.S. exchange rate system appeared to change over time with respect to the forecast variance. To examine the implications of this, we estimated the model over two subperiods. We then found that although the data were inconsistent with the theory in the first subperiod, the data were consistent with the theory in the second subperiod. Due to the complex nature of the restrictions, the cause of rejection could not be fully ascertained. In addition, although the theory may be rejected for Canada, there is no clear alternative theory that can be accepted.

CHAPTER IV

CONCLUSIONS

This dissertation has examined two dimensions of foreign exchange
market efficiency. First, an analysis of the relation between spot rates
and a one month forward rate was performed. Two methods were used to
analyze this aspect of efficiency. The first method was based on a regression of spot rates on lagged one month forward rates, corrected for the
serial correlation of the errors induced by using weekly data. The second
method is based on an explicit time series analysis of the spot rate and
one month forward rate. This method allows us to incorporate knowledge of
the (known) serial correlation properties of the forecast errors in the
estimation of the model. The empirical specification of the model enables
us to calculate an optimal (in the statistical sense) forecast of the future
spot rate using the stochastic structure of the model within the context of
the relevant economic theory. This statistical analysis, which is also applied to the term structure of the forward premium, is particularly useful
in studying economic dynamics; Thomas Sargent has usefully employed these
procedures in analyzing the term structure of interest rates (Sargent 1979),
the dynamics of the German hyperinflation (Salemi and Sargent 1977), estimation of dynamic labor demand schedules (Sargent 1978a and Hansen and
Sargent 1979), and the theory of the consumption function (Sargent 1978b).

The standard regression methods yielded results that were in some
cases favorable to the hypothesis of efficiency. It was found that the forward rate provided an unbiased forecast of the future spot rate for Canada,

Switzerland and the U.K., and a biased forecast for the Netherlands and Germany. However, we know that in a world with risk averse agents, the forward rate being an unbiased forecast of the future spot rate is neither necessary nor sufficient for market efficiency. What is required is that the forward rate summarize all available information relevant for forecasting the future spot rate. To test this aspect of efficiency an examination of the forecast errors, corrected for the structure of the model, was undertaken. It was found that for the Netherlands, Germany and Switzerland, the forward rate was efficient in this sense. For Canada and the U.K., it appears that currently available information could have been used to reduce the forecast errors.

The time series method yielded results that indicated rejection of market efficiency for all five currencies. Although it was not possible to determine the source of the rejection, examination of the sign pattern of the parameters provides some insight. We found that the "own" effects were negative while the "cross" effects were positive in the unrestricted and the restricted models. However, although the positive "cross" effects dominate the negative "own" effects in the unrestricted model, the negative "own" effects dominate the positive "cross" effects in the restricted (b=1) model. In addition, the effect of restricting the model by imposing b=1 was to cause the sum of the parameters in the s_t equation and the f_t equation to decline.

In Chapter III, we examined the implications of market efficiency for the joint movement of the spot rate and the one and six month forward rates. It was shown that the six month forward premium can be expressed as the geometric average of expected one month forward premiums. To add empirical content to this statement we must specify how expectations are

formed and what variables belong in the information set. To specify how
expectations are formed, we assumed that economic agents knew the stochastic
structure generating the one and six month forward premiums and the relevant economic theory--that is, expectations are rational. This assumption
restricts the parameters of the model in a highly nonlinear manner.

Two methods were used to test the validity of these restrictions.
The first method requires calculating only the unrestricted estimates. The
second method requires, in addition, calculating the restricted estimates.
It was found that the data were consistent with the theory for Germany, for
the whole period, and for Canada for the second subperiod. The data were
inconsistent with the theory for Canada for the whole period and the first
subperiod. The two methods, although asymptotically equivalent, are computationally quite different. In spite of this fact, the results were re-
markably close. In addition, the second method was approximately forty
times as expensive as the first method.

A number of questions remain unanswered and deserve consideration.
An important question is why did the two methods used in testing market
efficiency yield such different results? As Michael Jensen might argue,
the time series procedure developed is more sophisticated and hence we are
finding "inconsistencies that our cruder data and techniques missed in the
past" (Jensen 1978, p. 95). Also, it should be recalled that the results
may just indicate rejection of our particular characterization of market
efficiency, and not of market efficiency per se.

It was found in Chapter II that the slope coefficients were always
less than one, although not always significantly less than one. Is this a
statistical bias or does it reflect an (incorrect) specification of market
efficiency? To answer this question requires a more complete (and satis-

factory) specification of risk in the foreign exchange market. In addition, pooling currencies would conserve information concerning shocks common to all exchange rates (relative to the U.S. dollar). What are the special characteristics of the Swiss economy that cause the θ-vector to be significantly less than one, yet have the forecast errors be random?

A compelling question raised by this dissertation is how can these industrialized countries, which are closely connected through well integrated capital markets, exhibit signs of market inefficiencies? The answer to this fundamental question may be in expanding our equilibrium models to allow for more explicit consideration of a distinction between real and nominal shocks, transitory and permanent shocks, and the behavior of individual agents who have access only to incomplete information.

APPENDIX A

IMPLICATIONS OF USING WEEKLY AND MONTHLY DATA

In the text we assumed that one month is exactly four weeks. Of course, this is not the case. This appendix will examine the differences that arise from one month being approximately 4.3 weeks. In addition, this appendix will examine empirically the implications of using weekly data versus dropping three-fourths of the observations and using monthly data.

Consider Figure 1 which shows a "typical" calendar month. Assume, as we have been, that one month is exactly four weeks. Then, the (four week) forward rate set on Tuesday (x_1) is for delivery four weeks hence, on Tuesday (y). This data overlapping induces the MA(3) serial correlation. However, the data actually used is a one month forward rate, set on Tuesday (x_1) for delivery thirty days hence, on Thursday (x_2). The additional two days (y to x_2) induces additional serial correlation, so that we have an MA(4) process. Notice that if we look at $\ln S_{t+4} - \ln S_t$, we expect an MA(3) process, since we are comparing spot rates on Tuesdays (x_1 and y).

Sunday	Monday	Tuesday	Wednesday	Thursday	Friday	Saturday	
		x_1					Week 1
							Week 2
							Week 3
							Week 4
		y		x_2			Week 5

Fig. 1.--A typical calendar month

82

We can now discuss the empirical implications of using weekly data versus dropping three-fourths of the observations and using monthly data. Table 24 reports the results of estimating equation (2.1') with non-overlapping data. In this case, there is no problem with serial correlation so the parameter estimates are efficient. For each country, four regressions are reported, corresponding to using the first week of each month, second week of each month, etc. We see that the parameter estimates are similar to those reported in Table 6. The standard errors of the estimates are slightly larger in Table 24 than Table 6; this is what we expect since Table 6 uses four times as many observations. However, the improvement in precision is not great. A possible explanation is that we do not have four times as many "independent" observations since the spot and forward rates are very highly correlated.

84

TABLE 24

OLS ESTIMATION USING NONOVERLAPPING DATA

$$\ln S_{t+4} = a + b \ln F_t + u_{t+4}$$

(April 1973 – May 1977)

Country	Period	a	b	R^2	s.e.
Netherlands	Week 1	-0.184 (0.078)	0.806 (0.081)	.68	.027
	2	-0.269 (0.084)	0.717 (0.087)	.59	.030
	3	-0.265 (0.095)	0.722 (0.099)	.54	.033
	4	-0.255 (0.087)	0.733 (0.090)	.59	.030
Germany	Week 1	-0.240 (0.083)	0.737 (0.090)	.59	.029
	2	-0.305 (0.090)	0.667 (0.098)	.50	.033
	3	-0.250 (0.096)	0.728 (0.105)	.51	.034
	4	-0.285 (0.089)	0.689 (0.097)	.52	.032
Canada	Week 1	0.001 (0.001)	0.857 (0.087)	.67	.012
	2	0.001 (0.002)	0.879 (0.088)	.68	.012
	3	0.002 (0.001)	0.858 (0.070)	.76	.009
	4	0.001 (0.001)	0.889 (0.080)	.73	.011
Switzerland	Week 1	-0.071 (0.043)	-0.926 (0.043)	.91	.028
	2	-0.105 (0.052)	-0.892 (0.052)	.86	.035
	3	-0.080 (0.050)	0.918 (0.050)	.88	.033
	4	-0.082 (0.049)	0.916 (0.049)	.88	.032
United Kingdom	Week 1	0.005 (0.019)	0.990 (0.025)	.97	.024
	2	0.006 (0.019)	0.986 (0.025)	.97	.023
	3	0.012 (0.021)	0.978 (0.028)	.96	.026
	4	0.013 (0.022)	0.977 (0.029)	.96	.027

NOTES: Period i(i = 1, 2, 3, 4) refers to the ith week of the given month; with a monthly forward rate and one observation per month, there is no data overlap problem, consequently there is no serial correlation under the null hypothesis; s.e. refers to the standard error of the regression.

APPENDIX B

FUNCTIONAL FORMS IN TESTING MARKET EFFICIENCY

A serious econometric issue is what is the "correct" regression to use in testing efficiency. In the past, there have been at least three methods proposed. One is to run

$$S_{t+1} = a_1 + b_1 F_t + u_{t+1}. \tag{B.1}$$

This has been used by Frenkel (1978), Levich (1977) and others. An alternative is to regress the rate of depreciation on the forward premium:

$$S_{t+1} - S_t = a_2 + b_2(S_t - F_t) + v_{t+1}. \tag{B.2}$$

Bilson (1979), Tryon (1979) both advocate this equation. Finally, one can examine the forecast errors:

$$S_{t+1} - F_t = a_3 + b_3(S_t - F_{t-1}) + \dot{w}_{t+1}. \tag{B.3}$$

This method has been used by Stockman (1978), Geweke and Feige (1978) and Hansen and Hodrick (1979). Equations (B.1) and (B.2) are usually examined to test for a risk premium or bias in forecasting. Equation (B.3) is concerned solely with the information contained in the forecast errors. We shall focus on equations (B.1) and (B.2).

Rational expectations argues that in the regression

$$S_{t+1} = \alpha_1 + \beta_1 E_t S_{t+1} + \mu_{t+1} \tag{B.4}$$

85

we should expect to find $\alpha_1 = 0$ and $\beta_1 = 1$. If $F_t = E_t S_{t+1}$ and we substitute this into (B.4), we will obtain efficient estimates of α_1 and β_1 [in (B.4)] from running (B.1). Suppose, however, that $F_t = E_t S_{t+1} + n_t$, where n_t is a measurement error (see Obstfeld 1978). This could arise if expectations are heterogeneous and if equation (B.4) holds for the individual and F_t is a market variable. If we substitute $F_t - n_t$ for $E_t S_{t+1}$ in (B.4), then running (B.1) will yield biased estimates of α_1 and β_1 in (B.4). The bias can be shown to equal

$$BIAS_{(1)} = -\frac{\beta_1 \sigma_n^2}{\beta_F^2}.$$

Now consider an alternative characterization of the rational expectations hypothesis:

$$S_{t+1} - S_t = \alpha_2 + \beta_2(E_t S_{t+1} - S_t) + v_{t+1}. \tag{B.5}$$

In (B.5), we would expect to find $\alpha_2 = 0$ and $\beta_2 = 1$. If $\beta_1 = 1$ in (B.4), then we expect $\beta_2 = 1$ in (B.5) and that (B.4) and (B.5) are equivalent. As before, $E_t S_{t+1}$ is unobserved and we must use a "noisy" proxy, namely F_t. Therefore, substituting $F_t - S_t$ for $E_t S_{t+1} - S_t$ in (B.5) and running equation (B.2), will yield biased estimates of α_2 and β_2. As before, the bias can be shown to equal

$$BIAS_{(2)} = -\frac{\beta_2 \sigma_n^2}{\sigma_{(F-S)}^2}.$$

Without knowing the variance of the measurement error (σ_n^2), one cannot determine the extent or magnitude of the bias. However, one can determine the _relative_ bias. Assuming $\beta_1 = 1 = \beta_2$, then

$$\frac{\text{BIAS}_{(1)}}{\text{BIAS}_{(2)}} = \frac{\sigma^2_{(F-S)}}{\sigma^2_F} = \frac{\sigma^2_F + \sigma^2_S - 2\rho\sigma_F\sigma_S}{\sigma^2_F}.$$

Empirically we find σ^2_F and σ^2_S to be approximately equal and ρ (correlation between F_t and S_t) to be close to 1. Therefore, the bias in estimating β_1 (or β_2) from using (B.1) will be much less than the bias from using (B.2).

Of course, if we find $\beta_1 \neq 1$ then we would expect to find $\beta_2 \neq 1$. If $\sigma^2_\eta = 0$, that is, $F_t = E_t S_{t+1}$, and $b_1 = 1$ we expect to find $b_2 = 1$. Suppose $b_1 \neq 1$ (and $\sigma^2_\eta = 0$). Then, subtracting S_t from both sides of (B.1) yields

$$S_{t+1} - S_t = a_1 + b_1(F_t - S_t) + [(b_1 - 1)S_t + u_{t+1}]. \tag{B.6}$$

Therefore, running (B.2) as an OLS regression will yield biased estimates since $E\{(F_t - S_t)[(b_1 - 1)S_t + u_{t+1}]\} \neq 0$.

Similarly (see Tryon 1979), assume (B.2) is correct. Rearranging yields

$$S_{t+1} = a_2 + b_2 F_t + (1-b_2)S_t + v_{t+1}.$$

Assume there is the following (auxiliary) relation between S_t and F_t:

$S_t = cF_t + w_t$. Substituting this into the above equation yields

$$S_{t+1} = a_2 + \gamma F_t + [(1-b)w_t + v_{t+1}]$$

$$\gamma = b_2 + (1-b_2)c. \tag{B.7}$$

Now, γ can equal 1 if $b_2 = 1$ or if $c = 1$. We know that c is close to 1 so that γ is "biased" towards 1.

There is a final statistical argument. If, in doing hypothesis testing, we must rely on asymptotic results, then a common assumption to be made is that the variables are stationary stochastic process. As we saw earlier, $\ln S_t$ and $\ln F_t$ are non-stationary, and so equation (B.1) may be questionable. The first difference transformation will, in general, induce stationarity, and its effects on the time series properties of the variables are known. Therefore, first differencing equaton (B.1) may be appropriate. Note, however, that in general this will not lead to equation (B.2). It is true that the left hand and right hand sides of (B.2) are stationary, but the variables of (B.2) are not as nicely related to those of (B.1) as the first differences variables are. The transformation from (B.1) to (B.2) cannot be as simply analyzed as the transformation from (B.1) to the first difference of (B.1) can be analyzed.

Besides the econometric choice of using (B.1) or (B.2) to test the hypothesis of rational expectations, thre is an economic choice of which is the "true" relation. The economic behavior being described by the hypothesis $a_1 = 0$, $b_1 = 1$ is different from that being described by $a_2 = 0$, $b_2 = 1$. In (B.1) we can imagine an importer receiving foreign goods who is interested in the future price of the good; he would like an unbiased estimate of that future price. In (B.2) we can imagine a currency speculator trying to predict the total return for holding foreign currency relative to domestic currency (this is considering (B.2) in log form). He would like an unbiased estimate of that return. In one case we are led to look at $a_1 = 0$, $b_1 = 1$; in the other case, we are led to look at $a_2 = 0$, $b_2 = 1$.

APPENDIX C

INTERPRETATION OF THE θ-VECTOR IN TESTING

MARKET EFFICIENCY

Testing market efficiency, using standard regression methods, requires an analysis of the properties of the error term. In this appendix we shall present two alternative interpretations of the error term.

In the first interpretation, we show formally that θ_j can be expressed in terms of the variance of the change in our forecast of u_{t+4}. Given I_t and equation (2.11"), one can calculate u_t by assuming $\theta(L)$ is invertible and recalling that $u_t = \theta(L)^{-1}(\ln S_t - a - b\ln F_{t-4})$. By calculating $E_{t+j} \ln S_{t+4}$ from equation (2.1") it can be shown that (for $j = 1, 2, 3$)

$$E_{t+j}\ln S_{t+4} = E_{t+j-1}\ln S_{t+4} + \theta_j \varepsilon_{t+4-j}$$

That is, $\theta_j \varepsilon_{t+4-j}$ is the forecast revision, as a result of new information at time $t+j$. If we interpret ε_{t+4-j} as the shock to the system at time $t+j$, then θ_j is the weight attached to the shock used for revising our forecast. Recalling that $\varepsilon_{t+4} = u_{t+4} - E_{t+3}u_{t+4}$, and $u_{t+4} = \theta(L)\varepsilon_{t+4}$, it can be shown that

$$\theta_j = \left[\frac{\mathrm{Var}(E_{t+4-j}u_{t+4} - E_{t+4-j-1}u_{t+4})}{\mathrm{Var}(u_{t+4} - E_{t+3}u_{t+4})}\right]^{1/2}.$$

That is, after normalizing by the (constant) variance of the weekly shocks ($\sigma_\varepsilon^2 = \mathrm{Var}(u_{t+4} - E_{t+3}u_{t+4})$), θ_j^2 is equal to the variance of the change in

89

our forecast between $t+4-j-1$ and $t+4-j$, of u_{t+4}.

In the second interpretation, we make use of the bivariate stochastic process that is assumed to generate s_t and f_t. Given that we wish to impose the assumption that f_t summarizes all information (that is, equation (1') is correct), we can interpret the θ's of equation (2.1") in terms of the parameters of the time series process for s_t and f_t. Recalling that $s_t = \ln S_t - \ln S_{t-1}$ and $f_t = \ln F_t - \ln F_{t-1}$, we can define z_{t+4}, the forecast error, as follows:

$$
\begin{aligned}
z_{t+4} &= s_{t=4} - E_t s_{t+4} \\
&= \ln S_{t+4} - \ln S_{t+3} - E_t(\ln S_{t+4} - \ln S_{t+3}) \\
&= (\ln S_{t+4} - E_t \ln S_{t+4}) - (\ln S_{t+3} - E_t \ln S_{t+3}) \\
&= (\varepsilon_{t+4} + \theta_1 \varepsilon_{t+3} + \theta_2 \varepsilon_{t+2} + \theta_1 \varepsilon_{t+1}) - (\varepsilon_{t+3} + \theta_1 \varepsilon_{t+2} + \theta_2 \varepsilon_{t+1}) \\
&= \varepsilon_{t+4} + (\theta_1 - 1)\varepsilon_{t+3} + (\theta_2 - \theta_1)\varepsilon_{t+2} + (\theta_1 - \theta_2)\varepsilon_{t+1} \\
&\equiv \varepsilon_{t+4} + \phi_1 \varepsilon_{t+3} + \phi_2 \varepsilon_{t+2} + \phi_3 \varepsilon_{t+1}
\end{aligned}
$$

since $E_t \ln S_{t+3} = a + b \ln F_{t-1} + \theta_3 \varepsilon_t$ [from equation (2.1")]. Now, decompose the forecast error as follows:

$$
\begin{aligned}
s_{t+4} - E_t s_{t+4} &= \alpha(L)w_{t+4} + \beta(L)v_{t+4} - b(\gamma(L)w_t + \delta(L)v_t) \\
&= \alpha_0 w_{t+4} + \alpha_1 w_{t+3} + \alpha_2 w_{t+2} + \alpha_3 w_{t+1} + \left[\frac{\alpha(L)}{L^4}\right]_+ w_t \\
&\quad + \beta_0 v_{t+4} + \beta_1 v_{t+3} + \beta_2 v_{t+2} + \beta_3 v_{t+1} + \left[\frac{\beta(L)}{L^4}\right]_+ v_t \\
&\quad - b\gamma(L)w_t - b\delta(L)v_t \\
&= (\alpha_0 w_{t+4} + \beta_0 v_{t+4}) + (\alpha_1 w_{t+3} + \beta_1 v_{t+3}) \\
&\quad + (\alpha_2 w_{t+2} + \beta_2 v_{t+2}) + (\alpha_3 w_{t+1} + \beta_3 v_{t+1}).
\end{aligned}
\tag{C.1}
$$

Define $z_{t+4} = s_{t+4} - E_t s_{t+4}$ from equation (2.1). Letting $c(\tau)$ denote the covariogram of z_t, that is, $c(\tau) = E z_t z_{t-\tau}$, we have that

$$c(0) = \sigma_w^2(1 + \sigma_1^2 + \sigma_2^2 + \sigma_3^2) + \sigma_v^2(\beta_1^2 + \beta_2^2 + \beta_3^2) + 2\sigma_{wv}(\alpha_1\beta_1 + \alpha_2\beta_2 + \alpha_3\beta_3)$$

$$c(1) = \sigma_w^2(\alpha_1 + \alpha_1\alpha_2 + \alpha_2\alpha_3) + \sigma_v^2(\beta_1\beta_2 + \beta_2\beta_3) + \sigma_{wv}(\beta_1 + \beta_1\alpha_2 + \alpha_a\beta_2$$

$$+ \beta_2\beta_3 + \alpha_2\beta_3)$$

(C.2)

$$c(2) = \sigma_w^2(\alpha_2 + \alpha_1\alpha_3) + \sigma_v^2(\beta_1\beta_3) + \sigma_{wv}(\beta_2 + \beta_1\alpha_3 + \alpha_1\beta_3)$$

$$c(3) = \sigma_w^2(\alpha_3) + \sigma_{wv}(\beta_3)$$

$$c(s) = 0 \text{ for all } s > 5.$$

We want to find ϕ_1, ϕ_2, ϕ_3 and σ^2 such that $z_{t+4} = \varepsilon_{t+4} + \phi_1\varepsilon_{t+3} + \phi_2\varepsilon_{t+2}$ $+ \phi_3\varepsilon_{t+1}$ and $\text{var}(\varepsilon_t) = \sigma_\varepsilon^2$ [see equation (3')]. The autocovariogram of z_t, as defined here, is

$$c(0) = (1 + \phi_1^2 + \phi_2^2 + \phi_3^2)\sigma_\varepsilon^2$$

$$c(1) = (\phi_1 + \phi_1\phi_2 + \phi_2\phi_3)\sigma_\varepsilon^2$$

$$c(2) = (\phi_2 + \phi_1\phi_3)\sigma_\varepsilon^2$$

(C.3)

$$c(3) = \phi_3\sigma_\varepsilon^2$$

$$c(s) = 0 \text{ for all } s > .5.$$

Equating equations (C.2) and (C.3) gives us four nonlinear equations in the four unknowns ϕ_1, ϕ_2, ϕ_3 and σ_ε^2, which could be solved for $\phi_1 = \theta_1(\alpha_0, \alpha_1, \alpha_2, \alpha_3, \beta_0, \beta_1, \beta_2, \beta_3, \sigma_w^2, \sigma_v^2, \sigma_{wv})$. In general there will be many solutions only one of which will generate roots of $\theta(z) = 0$ being outside the unit circle.

Notice that we can rewrite (C.1) as

$$\theta(L)\varepsilon_{t+4} = \alpha'(L)w_{t+4} + \beta'(L)v_{t+4}$$

where
$$\alpha'(L) = \alpha_0 + \alpha_1 L + \alpha_2 L^2 + \alpha_3 L^3$$

$$\beta'(L) = \beta_0 + \beta_1 L + \beta_2 L^2 + \beta_3 L^3.$$

Therefore, by choosing the θ's such that $\theta(L)$ is invertible, we have that

$$\varepsilon_{t+4} = \frac{\alpha'(L)}{\phi(L)} w_{t+4} + \frac{\beta'(L)}{\phi(L)} v_{t+4}. \tag{C.4}$$

We see, therefore, that ε_{t+4} will be an infinite sum of lagged one-step ahead forecast errors.[1]

---

[1] It is interesting to note that ε_{t+4}, which is white noise, can be expressed as the sum of two highly autocorrelated random processes.

APPENDIX D

ALTERNATIVE FILTERS

In this appendix, we consider the question: What if first differencing is not the appropriate filter to induce stationarity? We provide a general procedure that can be generally used. In Chapter III we showed that the hypothesis of rational expectations implies the following restriction:

$$r_{n,t} = \frac{1}{n} [r_{1,t} + E_t r_{1,t+1} + \ldots + E_t r_{1,t+n-1}]. \tag{D.1}$$

Projecting both sides of (D.1) against θ_{t-1} (lagged values of $r_{1,t}$, $r_{n,t}$) we get

$$E(r_{n,t}|\theta_{t-1}) = \frac{1}{n} [E(r_{1,t}|\theta_{t-1}) + \ldots + E(r_{1,t+n-1}|\theta_{t-1})]. \tag{D.2}$$

Wold's decomposition theorem lets us express $\{r_{1,t}, r_{n,t}\}$ as the sum of a deterministic and linearly indeterministic part. Assume we can write $\{r_{1,t}, r_{n,t}\}$ as follows:

$$r_{1,t} = \sum_{i=1}^{M} \alpha_i r_{1,t-i} + \sum_{i=1}^{M} \beta_i r_{n,t-i} + c_1 + \tau_{11} t + \tau_{21} t^2 + a_{1,t}$$

$$\tag{D.3}$$

$$r_{n,t} = \sum_{i=1}^{M} \gamma_i r_{1,t-i} + \sum_{i=1}^{M} \delta_i r_{n,t-i} + c_n + \tau_{1n} t + \tau_{2n} t^2 + a_{n,t}.$$

Notice that the α, β, γ, δ will be different than those in Chapter III. Let us also define the new vector x_t and the new matrix A:

93

$$
x_t = \begin{bmatrix} r_{1,t} \\ r_{1,t-1} \\ \vdots \\ r_{1,t-M+1} \\ r_{n,t} \\ r_{n,t-1} \\ \vdots \\ r_{n,t-M+1} \\ 1 \\ t \\ t^2 \end{bmatrix}
$$

$$
A = \begin{bmatrix}
\alpha_1 & \cdots & \alpha_M & \beta_1 & \cdots & \beta_M & c_1 + \tau_{11} + \tau_{21} & \tau_{11} + 2\tau_{21} & \tau_{21} \\
1 & \cdots & 0 & 0 & \cdots & 0 & 0 & 0 & 0 \\
\vdots & & \vdots & \vdots & & \vdots & \vdots & \vdots & \vdots \\
0 & \cdots & 1\ 0 & 0 & \cdots & 0 & 0 & 0 & 0 \\
\gamma_1 & \cdots & \gamma_M & \delta_1 & \cdots & \delta_M & c_n + \tau_{1n} + \tau_{2n} & \tau_{1n} + 2\tau_{2n} & \tau_{2n} \\
0 & \cdots & 0 & 1 & \cdots & 0 & 0 & 0 & 0 \\
\vdots & & \vdots & \vdots & & 0 & 0 & 0 & 0 \\
0 & \cdots & 0 & 0 & 1 & 0 & 0 & 0 & 0 \\
0 & & \cdots & & & 0 & 1 & 0 & 0 \\
0 & & \cdots & & & 0 & 1 & 1 & 0 \\
0 & & \cdots & & & 0 & 1 & 2 & 1
\end{bmatrix} .
$$

We can now rewrite (D.3) as

$$x_t = Ax_{t-1} + a_t.$$

(D.4)

Defining c and d as before, and following the same steps as before, we get the following restrictions:

$$dA = \frac{1}{n} c[A + A^2 + \ldots + A^5].$$

(D.5)

Again, it should be stressed that this matrix A is different than the matrix A of Chapter III.

It is possible to partition the matrix A as

$$A = \begin{bmatrix} A_{11} & A_{12} \\ & \\ Z & A_{22} \end{bmatrix} \quad \begin{array}{l} A_{11} \text{ is M x M} \\ A_{12} \text{ is M x 3} \\ A_{22} \text{ is 3 x 3} \\ Z \quad \text{is 3 x M matrix of zeroes.} \end{array}$$

Using this partition we can rewrite (D.5) as

$$(\gamma_1\gamma_2 \cdots \gamma_M \delta_1\delta_2 \cdots \delta_M c_n + \pi_{1n} + \pi_{2n} \pi_{1n} + 2\pi_{2n} \pi_{2n}) =$$

$$\frac{1}{n} c \begin{bmatrix} A_{11} + A_{11}^2 + \ldots + A_{11}^5 & B \\ & \\ Z & A_{22} + A_{22}^2 + \ldots + A_{22}^5 \end{bmatrix}$$

(D.6)

where $B = A_{12}\{A_{11}^4 + A_{11}^3[A_{22} + I] + A_{11}^2[A_{22}^2 + A_{22} + I] + A_{11}[A_{22}^3 + A_{22}^2 + A_{22} + I] + [A_{22}^4 + A_{22}^3 + A_{22}^2 + A_{22} + I]\}$. Or, if we are interested in just the γ's and δ's, we can write

$$(\gamma_1, \ldots, \gamma_M, \delta_1, \ldots, \delta_M) = \frac{1}{n} c[A_{11} + A_{11}^2 + A_{11}^3 + A_{11}^4 + A_{11}^5].$$

(D.6')

We see, therefore, that the coefficients in the indeterministic part of the

$r_{n,t}$ autogression $(\gamma_1, \ldots, \gamma_M, \delta_1, \ldots, \delta_M)$ are highly nonlinear functions of the α's and β's—independent of the coefficients of the deterministic part (c's and τ's). That is, equation (D.6) defines the two (set) functions Ψ_1 and Ψ_2:

$$(\gamma, \delta) = \Psi_1(\alpha, \beta)$$

$$(c_1, c_n, \tau_{11}, \tau_{21}, \tau_{1n}, \tau_{2n}) = \Phi(\alpha, \beta, \gamma, \delta) = \Phi[\alpha, \beta, \psi_1(\alpha, \beta)] = \Psi_2(\alpha, \beta).$$

To estimate (D.3) subject to (D.2), we proceed as in the last section. First, estimate (D.3) unconstrained. Then, using these (consistent) OLS estimates in A_{11} in (D.6'), we iterate to constrained estimates of γ and δ that obey (D.6'). They will also obey the restriction (D.6) since we saw that we could write $(\gamma, \delta) = \psi_1(\alpha, \beta)$. Consequently, we can maximize the likelihood function with respect to α and β, calculating γ and δ using $_1$, then calculating the c's and τ's using Φ (equivalently ψ_2).

REFERENCES

Amemiya, Takeshi. "Generalized Least Squares with an Estimated Autoco-
variance Matrix." Econometrica 41 (July 1973): 723-732.

Anderson, T. W. The Statistical Analysis of Time Series. New York:
John Wiley and Sons, Inc., 1971.

Bilson, John F. O. "Forward and Future Exchange Rates: Is There a Relationship?" Unpublished manuscript, University of Chicago,
April 1979.

_____. "The 'Speculative Efficiency' Hypothesis." Unpublished
manuscript, University of Chicago, August 1979.

Bilson, John F. O. and Levich, Richard M. "A Test of the Forecasting
Efficiency of the Forward Exchange Rate." Unpublished manuscript, University of Chicago, June 1977.

Box, George E. P. and Jenkins, Gwilym M. Time Series Analysis: Forecasting and Control. San Francisco: Holden-Day, 1976.

Brillembourg, Arturo. "The Term Structure of Forward Rates." Unpublished
manuscript, International Monetary Fund, Washington, D.C., 1978.

Dooley, Michael P. and Shafer, Jeffrey R. "Analysis of Short-run Exchange
Rate Behavior: March 1973 to September 1975." International
Finance Discussion Paper, No. 76. Federal Reserve System,
Washington, D.C., February 1976.

Durbin, James. "Tests for Serial Correlation in Regression Analysis based
on the Periodogram of Least Squares Residuals." Biometrika 56
(1969): 1-15.

Fama, Eugene. "Efficient Capital Markets: A Review of Theory and Empirical Work." In Frontiers of Quantitative Economics. Edited
by Michael Intriligator. Amsterdam: North Holland Publishing
Company, 1971.

_____. "Short-term Interest Rates as Predictors of Inflation."
American Economic Review 65 (June 1975): 269-282.

_____. "Forward Rates as Predictors of Future Spot Rates." Journal
of Financial Economics 4 (October 1976): 361-377.

Fama, Eugene and Farber, Andre. "Money, Bonds and Foreign Exchange." Unpublished manuscript, University of Chicago, July 1978.

Frenkel, Jacob A. "A Monetary Approach to the Exchange Rate: Doctrinal Aspects and Empirical Evidence." _Scandanavian Journal of Economics_ 7, No. 2 (1976): 200-224.

_____. "The Forward Exchange Rate, Expectations, and the Demand for Money; The German Hyperinflation." _American Economic Review_ 67 (September 1977): 653-670.

_____. "International Reserves: Pegged Exchange Rates and Managed Float." Unpublished manuscript, University of Chicago, February 1978.

_____. "Further Evidence on Expectations and the Demand for Money during the German Hyperinflation." _Journal of Monetary Economics_ 5 (January 1979): 81-96.

Frenkel, Jacob A. and Clements, Kenneth. "Exchange Rates in the 1920's: A Monetary Approach." Report 7831, Center for Mathematical Studies in Business and Economics, University of Chicago, June 1978.

Frenkel, Jacob A. and Levich, Richard M. "Transaction Costs and Interest Arbitrage: Tranquil versus Turbulent Periods." _Journal of Political Economy_ 85 (December 1977): 1209-1226.

_____. "Covered Interest Arbitrage: Unexploited Profits?" _Journal of Political Economy_ 83 (April 1975): 325-338.

Friedman, Milton. "The Case for Flexible Exchange Rates." In _Essays in Positive Economics_. Chicago: University of Chicago Press, 1953.

Garber, Peter M. "Efficiency in Foreign Exchange Markets: Interpreting a Common Technique." Unpublished manuscript, University of Virginia, September 1978.

Geweke, John and Feige, Edgar. "Some Joint Tests of the Efficiency of Markets for Forward Foreign Exchange." Unpublished manuscript, No. 7804, University of Wisconsin, Madison, 1978.

Giddy, Ian H. "Term Structure and Expectations in the Money and Foreign Exchange Market." Unpublished manuscript, University of Chicago, March 1977.

Grauer, Frederick L. A.; Litzenberger, Robert H.; and Stahle, Richard E. "Sharing Rules and Equilibrium in an International Capital Market Under Uncertainty." _Journal of Financial Economics_ 3 (June 1976): 233-256.

Hannan, Edward J. "Regression for Time Series." In _Proceedings of a Symposium on Time Series Analysis_. Edited by Murray Rosenblatt. New York: John Wiley and Sons, 1963.

Hansen, Lars Peter. "The Symptotic Distribution of Least Squares Estimators with Endogenous Regressors and Dependent Residuals." Unpublished manuscript, Carnegie-Mellon University, March 1979.

Hansen, Lars Peter and Hodrick, Robert J. "Forward Exchange Rates as Optimal Predictors of Future Spot Rates: An Econometric Analysis." Unpublished manuscript, Carnegie-Mellon University, April 1979.

Hansen, Lars Peter and Sargent, Thomas J. "Formulating and Estimating Dynamic Linear Rational Expectations Models: I." Unpublished manuscript, Carnegie-Mellon University, March 1979.

Harris, Richard G. and Purvis, Douglas D. "Diverse Information and Market Efficiency in a Monetary Model of the Exchange Rate." Unpublished manuscript, Queen's University, June 1978.

Hatanaka, Michio. "An Efficient Two-Step Estimator for the Dynamic Adjustment Model with Autoregressive Errors." Journal of Econometrics 2 (September 1974): 199-220.

Hicks, J. R. Value and Capital. 2d ed. Oxford: Clarendon Press, 1968.

Jensen, Michael C. "Some Anomalous Evidence Regarding Market Efficiency." Journal of Financial Economics 6 (January 1978): 95-101.

Kessel, Reuben. The Cyclical Behavior of the Term Structure of Interest Rates. National Bureau of Economic Research Occasional Paper 91. New York: Columbia University Press, 1965.

Keynes, John M. A Tract on Monetary Reform. London: Macmillan and Co., Ltd., 1923.

Kohlhagen, Steven W. "The Foreign Exchange Markets--Models, Tests and Empirical Evidence." Unpublished manuscript, University of California, Berkeley, 1976.

Koopmans, L. R. The Spectral Analysis of Time Series. New York: Academic Press, 1974.

Kouri, Pentti. "The Determinants of the Forward Premium." Center for Research in Economic Growth, Memorandum No. 204, Stanford University, July 1976.

Krugman, Paul. "The Efficiency of the Forward Exchange Market: Evidence from the Twenties and the Seventies." Unpublished manuscript, Yale University, 1977.

Levich, Richard M. "The International Money Market." Ph.D. dissertation, University of Chicago, 1977.

_____. "Analyzing the Accuracy of Foreign Exchange Advisory Services: Theory and Evidence." Unpublished manuscript, New York University, February 1979. (a)

Levich, Richard M. "On the Efficiency of Markets for Foreign Exchange." In International Economic Policy. Edited by Rudiger Dornbusch and Jacob A. Frenkel. Baltimore: The Johns Hopkins University Press, 1979. (b)

Lucas, Robert E., Jr. "Econometric Policy Evaluation: A Critique." In The Phillips Curve and Labor Markets. Edited by Karl Brunner and Allan H. Meltzer. Carnegie-Rochester Conference Series on Public Policy. Supplementary series to Journal of Monetary Economics, Vol. I. Amsterdam: North-Holland, 1976.

_____. "Understanding Business Cycles." In Stabilization of the Domestic and International Economy. Edited by Karl Brunner and Allan H. Meltzer. Carnegie-Rochester Conference Series on Public Policy. Supplementary series to Journal of Monetary Economics, Vol. VII. Amsterdam: North-Holland, 1977.

Maddala, G. S. "Generalized Least Squares with an Estimated Variance Co-variance Matrix." Econometrica 39 (January 1971): 23-33.

Meiselman, David. The Term Structure of Interest Rates. Englewood Cliffs, N.J.: Prentice Hall, Inc., 1962.

Modigliani, Franco and Shiller, Robert J. "Inflation, Rational Expectations and the Term Structure of Interest Rates." Economica, N.S. 40 (February 1973):12-43.

Morrison, Donald F. Multivariate Statistical Methods. New York: McGraw-Hill Book Company, 1967.

Mussa, Michael. "Empirical Regularities in the Behavior of Exchange Rates and Theories of the Foreign Exchange Market." Unpublished manuscript, University of Chicago, March 1979.

_____. "The Exchange Rate, the Balance of Payments, and Monetary and Fiscal Policy under a Regime of Controlled Floating." In The Economics of Exchange Rates: Selected Studies. Edited by Jacob A. Frenkel and Harry G. Johnson. Reading, Mass.: Addison-Wiley, 1978.

Muth, John F. "Rational Expectations and the Theory of Price Movements." Econometrica 29 (July 1961): 315-335.

Nelson, Charles. The Term Structure of Interest Rates. New York: Basic Books, Inc., 1972.

Obstfeld, Maurice. "Expectations and Efficiency in the Foreign Exchange Market." Unpublished manuscript, Massachusetts Institute of Technology, May 1978.

Poole, William. "Speculative Prices as Random Walks: An Analysis of Ten Time Series of Flexible Exchange Rates." The Southern Economic Journal 34 (April 1967): 468-478.

Porter, Michael G. "A Theoretical and Empirical Framework for Analyzing the Term Structure of Exchange Rate Expectations." IMF Staff Papers 18 (November 1971): 613-645.

Rao, C. R. Linear Statistical Inference and its Applications. 2d ed. New York: John Wiley and Sons, 1973.

Roll, Richard. "The Efficient Market Model Applied to the U.S. Treasury Bill Rates." Ph.D. dissertation, University of Chicago, 1968.

Roll, Richard and Solnick, Bruno. "On Some Parity Conditions Frequently Encountered in International Economics." Unpublished manuscript, University of Chicago, June 1977.

_____. "A Pure Foreign Exchange Asset Pricing Model." Journal of International Economics 7 (1977): 161-179.

Salemi, Michael and Sargent, Thomas J. "The Demand for Money During Hyper-inflation Under Rational Expectations: II." Unpublished manuscript, University of North Carolina, June 1977.

Sargent, Thomas J. "Rational Expectations and the Term Structure of Interest Rates." Journal of Money, Credit, and Banking 4 (February 1972): 74-97.

_____. "Estimation of Dynamic Labor Demand Schedules under Rational Expectations." Journal of Political Economy 86 (December 1978): 1009-1044. (a)

_____. "Rational Expectations, Econometric Exogeneity, and Consumption." Journal of Political Economy 86 (August 1978): 673-700. (b)

_____. Macroeconomic Theory. New York: Academic Press, 1979. (a)

_____. "A Note on Maximum Likelihood Estimation of the Rational Expectation Model of the Term Structure." Journal of Monetary Economics 5 (January 1979): 133-143. (b)

Silvey, S. D. Statistical Inference. New York: Chapman Hall, 1975.

Sims, Christopher A. "Are There Exogenous Variables in Short-Run Production Relations?" Annals of Economic and Social Measurement 1 (January 1972): 17-36.

Stockman, Alan C. "Risk, Information and Forward Exchange Rates." In The Economics of Exchange Rates: Selected Studies. Edited by Jacob A. Frenkel and Harry G. Johnson. Reading, Mass.: Addison-Wiley, 1978.

Telser, Lester G. "A Critique of Some Recent Empirical Research on the Explanation of the Term Structure of Interest Rates." Journal of Political Economy 75 (August 1967): 546-560.

Tryon, Ralph. "Testing for Rational Expectations in Foreign Exchange Markets." International Finance Discussion Papers, No. 139. Federal Reserve System, Washington, D.C., May 1979.

Tsiang, S. C. "The Theory of Forward Exchange and Effects of Government Intervention on the Forward Exchange Market." IMF Staff Papers 7 (April 1959): 75-106.

Whittle, Paul. Prediction and Regulation by Linear Least Square Methods. Princeton, N.J.: D. Van Nostrand Company, Inc., 1963.

Wilson, G. Tunnicliffe. "The Estimation of Parameters in Multivariate Time Series Models." Journal of the Royal Statistical Society B 35, No. 1 (1973): 76-85.

For Product Safety Concerns and Information please contact our
EU representative GPSR@taylorandfrancis.com Taylor & Francis
Verlag GmbH, Kaufingerstraße 24, 80331 München, Germany